Enrico Pescantini

Online Marketing and Hollywood

Promoting films on Internet in the U.S. Market

LAP LAMBERT Academic Publishing

Impressum/Imprint (nur für Deutschland/ only for Germany)

Bibliografische Information der Deutschen Nationalbibliothek: Die Deutsche Nationalbibliothek verzeichnet diese Publikation in der Deutschen Nationalbibliografie; detaillierte bibliografische Daten sind im Internet über http://dnb.d-nb.de abrufbar.

Alle in diesem Buch genannten Marken und Produktnamen unterliegen warenzeichen-, marken- oder patentrechtlichem Schutz bzw. sind Warenzeichen oder eingetragene Warenzeichen der jeweiligen Inhaber. Die Wiedergabe von Marken, Produktnamen, Gebrauchsnamen, Handelsnamen, Warenbezeichnungen u.s.w. in diesem Werk berechtigt auch ohne besondere Kennzeichnung nicht zu der Annahme, dass solche Namen im Sinne der Warenzeichen- und Markenschutzgesetzgebung als frei zu betrachten wären und daher von jedermann benutzt werden dürften.

Coverbild: www.ingimage.com

Verlag: LAP LAMBERT Academic Publishing GmbH & Co. KG
Dudweiler Landstr. 99, 66123 Saarbrücken, Deutschland
Telefon +49 681 3720-310, Telefax +49 681 3720-3109
Email: info@lap-publishing.com

Herstellung in Deutschland:
Schaltungsdienst Lange o.H.G., Berlin
Books on Demand GmbH, Norderstedt
Reha GmbH, Saarbrücken
Amazon Distribution GmbH, Leipzig
ISBN: 978-3-8443-3256-8

Imprint (only for USA, GB)

Bibliographic information published by the Deutsche Nationalbibliothek: The Deutsche Nationalbibliothek lists this publication in the Deutsche Nationalbibliografie; detailed bibliographic data are available in the Internet at http://dnb.d-nb.de.

Any brand names and product names mentioned in this book are subject to trademark, brand or patent protection and are trademarks or registered trademarks of their respective holders. The use of brand names, product names, common names, trade names, product descriptions etc. even without a particular marking in this works is in no way to be construed to mean that such names may be regarded as unrestricted in respect of trademark and brand protection legislation and could thus be used by anyone.

Cover image: www.ingimage.com

Publisher: LAP LAMBERT Academic Publishing GmbH & Co. KG
Dudweiler Landstr. 99, 66123 Saarbrücken, Germany
Phone +49 681 3720-310, Fax +49 681 3720-3109
Email: info@lap-publishing.com

Printed in the U.S.A.
Printed in the U.K. by (see last page)
ISBN: 978-3-8443-3256-8

Table of Contents

I. Introduction

The motion picture industry is an interesting business from several different points of view. From a macroeconomic perspective, entertainment is the United States' main export market, and film industry employs over half a million people, with a 2007 box office income of $9.6 billion in the USA and $26.7 billion all over the world (MPAA, 2008), revenues that seem to have a positive growth rate.

From a researching side, motion picture industry is a fascinating subject of investigation: films have an interesting double nature, being at the same time art products and economic products (Salvemini S. , 1992; Salvemini & Soda, Artwork & Network, 2001; Salvemini S. , Il cinema impresa possibile, 2002). And due to this economic side, the motion picture industry is characterized by a wide and deep availability of data about the performance of films at the box office (and also in the secondary market); these fresh sources of data are often exploited by academics to perform a group of analysis that embraces a broad range of different disciplines, from economy to social and psychology studies

Analyzing the industry from a business perspective, the marketing of films seems to be one of the most important topics, due to the primary role that marketing plays in the film economics. To understand this role, it is necessary to start with a definition, here suggested by the American Marketing Association[1]:

"Marketing is an organizational function and a set of processes for creating, communicating, and delivering value to customers and for managing customer relationships in ways that benefit the organization and its stakeholders."

In the case of films, the value that marketing should create, communicate and deliver to customers is basically the information about the product, in order to help them during the purchase process that is particularly complex and performed under an uncertain en-

---

[1] http://www.marketingpower.com/_layouts/Dictionary.aspx?dLetter=M

vironment. This uncertainty is due first of all to the nature of the film of *experience good* (Nelson, 1970): in the consumer evaluation process a *search good* is a product which quality and reliability in satisfying the consumer's need can be predicted by its factual information; the *experience good* instead reveals its capability in satisfying the need only after the consumption, and for this reasons the purchase of an experience good requires more information than a search good, information that can be obtained through a costly research by the consumer or relying on the one provided by the marketing of the product. The unpredictability of films as experience goods is strengthen by another property, that is the "prototypal" nature of films (Celata & Caruso, 2003; Salvemini S. , 1992): while an industrial product is characterized at least by three stages of development (creation of the prototype, production of the pilot series and mass production), the film development process stops with the creation of a unique prototype, that is the result of the combination of several factors (actors, directors, plot, soundtrack, etc.) that cannot be re-assembled to reproduce the same final output. The consequence for consumers is the duty of performing a purchase decision on a product that cannot be easily compared with other products and that cannot be evaluated until the actual consumption.

This explains the strong need of information by the audience of films, which behavior is anyway different. Part of audience is willing to dedicate time and efforts in a personal research of information about the film: this is defined as primary audience (Pham & Watson, 1993; Celata & Caruso, 2003), and is composed by the segments of audience that represent the ideal target of the film (like for example teens for horror movies or children for family animation movies). This core audience is probably going to watch the film in any case, so the only marketing effort should aim in making available the information they need. The hard work comes with the secondary audience, which represents all the other segments of moviegoers that *may* be interested in watching the film but are not willing to invest any resources in searching information. Marketing plays a determinant role in this scenario, providing to potential consumers the information they need to reduce the uncertainty of the purchase and influencing their decision.

Along this evaluation process the consumer of film product is subjected to two pressures that may influence his purchasing decision: the internal and external competition. The internal competition refers to the different occasion of consumption of the film product: besides watching film in theatres (also called primary market), audience can choose to rent or buy the DVD, buy the film on pay-per-view television or watch it on subscription or free television (all referred as secondary market)[2]; even if secondary markets have extended the revenues' lifespan of films, they have also contributed to increase the competitive pressure within the industry. The external competition instead involves other products of entertainment industry, such as theatres plays and musicals, sport games and amusement parks, that all compete for the same share of expenses which consumers dedicate to leisure and free time.

Established the crucial role of marketing in the motion picture industry, it is possible to observe that this function actually involves a wide range of different tools and media, like for example:

- In-Theatres Advertising;
- Radio commercials;
- TV commercials;
- Print advertising;
- Billboards;
- Events and News releases;
- Online Marketing.

Of all these, this analysis will concentrate on the most recent and revolutionary media: the Internet. There are several reasons why online marketing is worth of a specific and particular attention: Internet is the most recent and faster growing media of the ones above described, that makes it continuously changing and evolving. New tools and new technologies are implemented every day, making difficult for online marketing literature to follow this fast pace of changing: for example an online marketing book of a couple of years ago would not even consider social networking websites and not even *Facebook*, while now they have become a billion dollar business for marketing and advertising. Besides, the motion picture industry is characterized by a culture extremely resistant to changes and like all innovations, also the Internet and online marketing have been recognized by Hollywood studios only in the last few years.

---

[2] The film is available in the different channels in different intervals of time: the film is first release on theatres, then after X months on DVD rental and so on.

The importance of online marketing can be distinguished also through a quick overview of the most recent statistics and data of the motion picture industry. The report "2007 Movie Attendance Study" (MPAA, 2008) published by the Motion Picture Association of America states that of the 1.47 billion of U.S. admissions in the 2007, the age group of 12-24 years old led the ticket purchases, representing the 28% of all the admissions. Moreover, this same segment represents the 41% of all the frequent moviegoers[3]: these are impressive results since the 12-24 represents only the 22% of the total population of the United States:

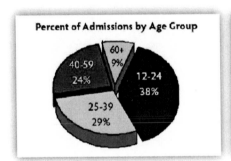 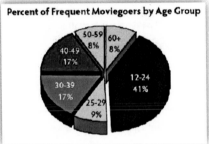

Figure 1 - Moviegoers Demographics (MPAA, 2008)

The conclusion is that the most profitable demographic segment in the motion picture industry is on average the 12-24 years old one, and it should indeed represents the primary target of the marketing efforts. Of all the possible media where the promotional message could be deployed, Internet seems to be the most popular among young people, a trend that is confirmed by several sources. According to Pew Internet Project in 2007 the 90% of 18-29 years old were Internet users (PEW/INTERNET, 2008), a percentage that increases to 94% among the 12-18 years old; 63% of teenage internet users go online daily, and the 35% even multiple times a day (PEW/INTERNET, 2008). According to eMarketer (Williamson, College Students Online:, 2008) instead, in 2007 the 95% of

---

[3] MPAA defines frequent moviegoers as "a *person who sees at least one movie in a theater per month*".

college students were internet users, proof of an extremely strong Internet penetration among these segments of population.

But the Internet diffusion is not limited to the youngest segments of U.S. population. In the update of October 2008 (Phillips L. , 2008), eMarketer estimates that in 2008 the US Internet population was of 192.8 million of people, representing the 63.4% of the population, a penetration index that is forecasted to increase in the next years:

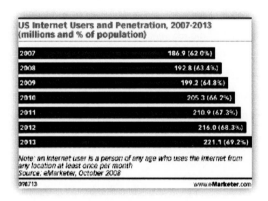

US Internet Users and Penetration, 2007-2013
(millions and % of population)

Year	Users (Penetration)
2007	186.9 (62.0%)
2008	192.8 (63.4%)
2009	199.2 (64.8%)
2010	205.3 (66.2%)
2011	210.9 (67.3%)
2012	216.0 (68.3%)
2013	221.1 (69.2%)

Note: an internet user is a person of any age who uses the internet from any location at least once per month
Source: eMarketer, October 2008

078713   www.eMarketer.com

Figure 2 - Internet Users and Penetration, 2007-2013 (Phillips L. , 2008)

The establishing of Internet as a major medium in the U.S. population is confirmed also in the MPAA data about the media consumption (MPAA, 2008) that report the average time spent by consumers on each medium. In the period 2003-2007 all traditional media (TV, radio and press) have recorded a progressive decline in the consumption, while consumer Internet recorded an impressive increase of 18.3%[4]. Even if the total hours spent on TV and radio are still three-four times the time spent on Internet (in 2007: 676 hours for TV, 769 hours for radio and 181 hours for Internet), this is an important trend that forecasts the evolution in the consumers' behavior in the next years.

---

[4] In particular, Broadcast TV changed of -7.3%, Broadcast & Satellite Radio of -7.8%, Newspapers of -11.8% and Consumer Magazines of -2.5%.

Like mentioned before, the role of marketing in motion picture industry is mainly to provide information to moviegoers, trying to influence their decisions. It has also been verified that among the media that marketing could exploit, Internet seems to be a rising star, with positive trends in the extension (indicated by the Internet penetration in the U.S. population) and in the deepness (hours spent on Internet) of the phenomenon. Different studies indeed have confirmed that Internet has become an extremely important source for searching information: the marketing research firm MarketCast (Thilk, Internet is where people go for movie information, 2006; Walsh, Google Study: Internet Directs Moviegoers, 2006) surveyed 2,100 moviegoers from 13 to 49 years old and the results were that the 70% of the moviegoers that actively conducted a research to find out information about a film used the Internet, and the 17% of the interviewed declared that the Internet research was the most important influencing factor in the selection of the film. Similar findings come from a study conducted by MPAA and Yahoo! (MPAA, 2008) which found that the 73% of the U.S. moviegoers use the Internet to conduct a research before going to the theatres:

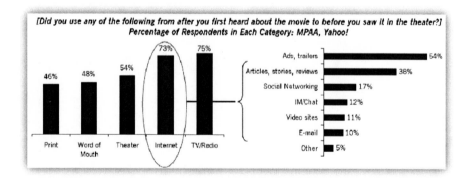

Figure 3 - Preferred Media for searching movie information - (MPAA, 2008)

In conclusion it is possible to draw some assumptions that will lead this analysis:

- The nature of films implies for the audience a strong need of information in order to perform the choice of purchase; the information can be obtained through research (that in expensive) or relying on movie marketing;

- Most of the audience chooses the Internet as primary source of information to decide which film watch in theatres, and is one of the most significant influencing factors;
- More Americans become Internet users, and they increase the time spent online rather than consuming other media; teens are the segment more addicted to the Web, and they also represent the more frequent moviegoers;
- Marketing online means at the same time:
    o reaching moviegoers that are online looking for information;
    o reaching moviegoers that are spending their free time surfing the Web;
    o reaching the segment of the frequent moviegoers: online teens.

This implies that implementing an online marketing campaign helps to achieve at the same time three objectives that lead to the final goal, which is convincing the audience to go to the theatres and watch the promoted film. The purpose of this analysis is indeed to give insights about the possible influence that the online marketing campaign could have on the moviegoing decision.

The study will start examining the different tools that could be utilized in an online marketing strategy, with a classification in nine categories. Definitions and a short description of each of them will provide the theoretical framework necessary to build the *Online Marketing Scorecard*: this combines quantitative and qualitative indicators for each marketing tool, trying to summarize the quality of the film marketing campaign in a unique score. This scorecard will be then applied to a sample of 66 films recently released in the U.S.A.[5] theatres in order to gain a better comprehension of dynamics such as the possible relationships between marketing campaign, budget and box office and between marketing tools and genre of films.

---

[5] The sample is composed by the films that were in the Top25 Box Office result from the weekend of August 8th to the weekend of October 10th, 2008.

II. Online Marketing Tools:
a theoretical background

Categorizing and analyzing online marketing tools is a task that presents different challenges. First of all, there is not any authoritative and established literature on these arguments: Internet spread into the mainstream audience only after 2000, so all online marketing is a very new topic. Besides, some of the tools analyzed have been introduced even more recently, like the social network *Facebook*, introduced in 2006, or the *iPhone* applications, that are dated 2008. For these reasons there are no accepted definitions and classifications for each tool, so the effort has been to summarize a stream of opinions and interpretations.

A second challenge is to classify each tool into a specific category: some of them could easily belong to more than one category, others (the official website for example) could instead work as folders for more tools. The following classification has not the purpose of suggesting a theoretical system of relationships between the existing online marketing tools, but only to provide a framework of tools that will be analyzed in the empirical analysis.

A final challenge is describing an argument that is constantly changing and evolving: new web technologies are introduced every month, and the existing one are often edited and updated. Instead of an exhaustive description, the following classification could be regarded as an instant photography of the status of the online marketing tools in this particular moment, a situation that ill probably change and evolve very soon.

This framework will introduce nine categories of online marketing tools, each of whom could include one or more tools.

1.1 Official Website

The official website is the first online marketing tool used by Hollywood to promote films. Before blogs, social networking websites and podcasts, film official websites were the only effort made by studios for providing information on the Internet. In particular after the astonishing results reached by *The Blair Witch Project*, a few thousands dollars horror film that thanks to the first online promotion campaign ever earned more than \$240 million[6], movie studios heavily invested on official movie websites, making them the centrepiece of their online marketing strategy.

In the last years, official websites have become folders for every kind of media content, like games, videos, contests, and new web technologies (like Flash[7]) made these websites truly virtual experiences. Besides a huge variety among film websites, there are some basic features that almost all of them presents, even if named in many different ways:

- *About the Film (or synopsis, story, the film)*: it is a short description of what the film is about, the concept behind it or every kind of information related to the film;
- *About the Cast and Filmmakers (or talent)*: in this section, website presents the cast, like actors, filmmakers and other people involved in the film production, with usually a biography, a filmography and some pictures;
- *Videos*: that could be from simple trailers and TV commercials to behind the scenes, film premieres, interviews with cast and filmmakers and so on;

---

[6] From *http://IMDb.com*.

[7] This is the definition from *http://searchcio-midmarket.techtarget.com*: "*Flash, a popular authoring software developed by Macromedia, is used to create vector graphics-based animation programs with full-screen navigation interfaces, graphic illustrations, and simple interactivity in an antialiased, resizable file format that is small enough to stream across a normal modem connection. The software is ubiquitous on the Web, both because of its speed (vector-based animations, which can adapt to different display sizes and resolutions, play as they download) and for the smooth way it renders graphics. Flash files, unlike animated but rasterized GIF and JPEG, are compact, efficient, and designed for optimized delivery.*"

- *Gallery (or images, pictures):* a gallery of images that could be screenshots from the movie, shots from the set, artworks, pictures of the cast and film-related events, etc.;
- *Downloadable Content:* users can almost always download some kind of film content to customize their computers or even mobile phones, and usually are wallpapers, screensavers, icons, cell ringtones etc.;
- *Extra (or features):* this is the category that could vary the most, and it could offer online games, some kind of *"send-to-your-friends"* viral content, widgets and any other "plus" to enrich the website's offering;
- *Links:* or through a specific section or through banners placed on the website layout, audience is invited to browse other film-related websites, like social networking pages (usually Facebook and\or MySpace), mobile content providers' websites, mini-sites created by the promotional partners, positive critics' reviews pages, fan websites, and so on.

A new feature recently used by a lot of blockbusters movies is a "welcome" page: after typing the web address, the user is linked to an intro page where, besides the link to the official website (that often opens in a new window build in Flash), other features are offered. The number of the features of the welcome page has lately grown to become a sort of synthesis of the extended official website, and usually there are the trailer (usually offered in different resolutions) with the option for the restricted version (in the case of mature content films), links to the social networks' pages (like *"Find us in Facebook"* or *"Join us on MySpace"*), contests or games or links to other film websites. A very new feature recently posted in film welcome pages is an iPhone button that links to an iPhone friendly version of the website: this is an excellent way to attract the growing segment of audience that surf the Internet through their smartphones.

Even if movie marketers heavily invest on official movie websites, this can not be considered anymore the centre and main tool of the online marketing strategy. With the advent of the Web 2.0 (O'Reilly, 2005) and the information democracy, studios and official websites are not the only information providers about film and actually they are not even the best ones. Film reviews websites like *Rotten Tomatoes*[8] or film portals like

---

[8] http://www.rottentomatoes.com/

Internet Movie Database[9] or fan communities like *Flixster[10]* have become the main reference for every movie infoseekers, reaching a strong and devoted users' base. Every time studios want to launch a film, they can't hope to reach a broader audience and generate so much traffic like those consolidated websites, but they have to realize (and admit) the lost of brand control, that now is up to the audience: pretending to be the publishers of every piece of content related to their film is like trying to swim upstream: it can't happen. Instead, studios should use their expertise and their resources to stimulate the audience, acknowledging its influence and let the fans help to spread the buzz. So the official website would be just a piece of the online marketing deployment, along with uploading trailers and clips on YouTube, creating pages on MySpace and Facebook, rewarding fan blogs and communities and so on. In this new multi-dimensional approach, the official website should become a sort of portal that links to all the other efforts on the Internet, a first step for the infoseekers providing them with the information and the content to become fans of the film and move on other websites, helping to spread the buzz.

So while official websites aspire to be info portals, they should also acknowledge the presence of a fan community that invests time and efforts to talk about their favourite film, writing on blogs, creating fan art, websites and so on. A great achievement would be dedicate a section of the website to these fans (Thilk, Movie Marketing and Consumer Control: Part 2, 2006; Thilk, Movie Marketing and Consumer Control: Part 3, 2006) and this could be accomplished through different tools: the more common ones are forums, discussion boards, chats, links to fan websites and *wikis*. *Wiki* is an Hawaiian word that means *fast* and was first used by Ward Cunningham[11] to describe online databases edited by the web community: the masterpiece of these collaborative websites is the free online encyclopaedia *Wikipedia[12]*. For what concerns movie marketing, *wikis* are created to provide users with information on the film's characters and events, and they are mainly used for sci-fi or fantasy films.

---

[9] http://www.imdb.com/

[10] http://www.flixster.com/

[11] http://en.wikipedia.org/wiki/Ward_Cunningham

[12] http://en.wikipedia.org/wiki/Wiki

Good examples of this community acknowledgement are the films *Munich* and *Poseidon*. Steven Spielberg's *Munich* has on its website[13] a Link page dedicated to all the websites that provides a background to the even narrated in the film, while the *Poseidon*'s website lists in the *Journals* section[14] the link banners of movie fans' websites that have published articles about the film.

The assessment of the film official website involves several different aspects, which could be anyway summarized in *content* and *look*. The content regards the core of the website, the quality and quantity of the information provided through the different sections; it should therefore be targeted to the core audience of the film, and designed from that perspective. The look concerns instead of the visual design of the website and how this matches with the look of the film. Film websites differ from other brand flagship websites, where the content represents the most important quality: film is a visual art and the website should offer a visual experience that shares the same emotions of the film, which could be described as consistency. A masterpiece of this concept is the official website for the Darren Aronofsky's *The Fountain*[15], an extreme sample of film-website consistency, where the films is introduced to the user through an interactive visual experience that fully recreates the emotions of the movie. The official film website should indeed maintain a balance between the content offered and how this content is offered to the audience and above all should not be conceived as the final destination of the user, but as a "launch station" into other tools of the online marketing strategy, triggering the initial interest about the film and begin the process of transform the info-seeker into a *fan*.

---

[13] http://www.munichmovie.com/main.html

[14] http://poseidonmovie.warnerbros.com/index2.html

[15] http://thefountainmovie.warnerbros.com/experience/index.html

User-generated content (also called consumer-generated media) can be generally defined as any kind of material that is uploaded on the Internet by non-professional users (Interactive Advertising Bureau, 2008). OECD suggested three criteria for identifying what is a user-generated content (OECD, 2007):

- *Publication Requirement*: the material created by the user has to be published on the Internet for an audience of people, which could be the whole Internet, if published on web pages or blogs, or a restricted group of people, like in social network websites. Therefore this definition excludes emails or instant messages.
- *Creative effort*: the user added through his creative work a recognizable value to the final output, a work than can either be modifying an existing content or creating a new one. The minimum amount of creative effort to define a UGC is an argument open to discussion: a significant contradiction is *YouTube*, that represents a UGC website for definition, but at the same time a lot of uploaded videos are just copied and pasted from other sources, with a clear lack any creative effort. It is anyway arguable that making available a video to a worldwide audience like the *YouTube* one could be considered as an added value to the original content.
- *Creation outside of professional routines and practises*: content should be created outside a commercial or institutional context, without expectations of profit or remuneration.

User-generated content is at the basis of the *participative web* (also called Web 2.0) (O'Reilly, 2005), that can be defined as an extended exploitation of the capacities of the Internet platform to amplify the interaction and the participation with and among users. A superior level of communication, a globally shared knowledge and enhanced web based technologies have contributed to the creation of a global boundary-free comnity. And according to E-Marketer, the size of UGC creators' community is constantly growing, reaching nearly half of the US internet users.

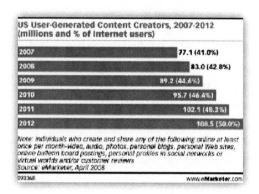

US User-Generated Content Creators, 2007-2012 (millions and % of Internet users)

Year	Value
2007	77.1 (41.0%)
2008	83.0 (42.8%)
2009	89.2 (44.6%)
2010	95.7 (46.4%)
2011	102.1 (48.2%)
2012	108.5 (50.0%)

Note: individuals who create and share any of the following online at least once per month–video, audio, photos, personal blogs, personal Web sites, online bulletin board postings, personal profiles in social networks or virtual worlds and/or customer reviews
Source: eMarketer, April 2008

093368   www.eMarketer.com

Figure 4 - US User-Generated Content Creators, 2007-2012

From a marketing perspective, UGC is usually embedded in marketing tools like contests and sweepstakes: in order to engage this community brands often launches promotional contests where the best UGC wins some kind of prize. Film studios have recognized UGC contests as powerful tools to promote films online and for achieving at the same time multiple goals: they engage passionate fans, they help to raise and spread a positive Word of Mouth and they generally have a positive ROI, since all the creative efforts are produced by the audience, and the studio usually provides only the platform, some guidelines and rewards.

Rewards could be extremely different: special editions of DVDs, tickets to the film premiere, memorabilia and collectibles from the film, money, opportunities to meet the cast and so on. Perhaps one of the most valuable prizes is the acknowledgement of the creative content produced by fans: a good example of engaging and involving audience in the creation of the marketing campaign of a film is the promotion of the horror film *Slither*. Universal Studios launched on the official website a contest called *Slug it out*[16] where the studio made available online a variety of video and audio material from the film that users could use for creating their own TV spot. Beyond DVDs and money, the winner re-

---

[16] http://www.slithermovie.net/slugitout/makespot.php

ceived the possibility to have his spot aired during the TV promotional campaign of the film, gaining his 30 seconds of popularity.

A first method to evaluate the success of a UGC contest could be the number of entries that have been submitted but, even it is usually available, it measures only the direct engagement of the audience. Besides the users that submit their creative work to the contest, the analysis should also take into consideration the indirect engagement of the audience, which is the word of mouth generated by the contest, like entries in blogs, media coverage and so on. Since the word of mouth can not be easily measured, the number of entries could be a quantitative start for the analysis of the success of a user-generated content contest.

2. Social Networking Websites

According to the definition provided by Danah M. Boyd and Nicole B. Ellison in the whitepaper *"Social Network Sites: definition, history and scholarships"* (Boyd & Ellison, 2007), a social network website is a web-based service that allow individuals to:

- create a profile within the website that can be public or private. The profile is the virtual representation of the user, which defines his identity online;
- search and link with other users with whom they share a connection; in order to publicly establish a connection there usually must be an approval from the other user;
- browse through these lists of connection, in order to explore the web of links.

Beyond these three principles, each websites can have a wide differentiation of features (PC Magazine; Bhopu, 2007; Owyang, Social Networking). Profiles usually displays biographical information, activities, interests, groups of affiliation and a range of multimedia content, from pictures to videos to music. A common feature of these websites is also a kind of messaging system, that can range from private messages, public ones (like comments) or instant messaging services (the "chat"). Great variety involves also the privacy settings: usually users have a strong control of what can be publicly seen and what not, from the profile to the list of friends to the public listing in search engines.

The first recognized social network website was *SixDegrees.com*, launched by Andrew Weinreich (Bedell, 1998) in 1997, that combined for the first time all the features of a social network website, such as a list of Friends, the possibility to browse through them and a messaging system. As the founder himself admitted, it was probably ahead its time and the website closed in 2000. The next milestone in the social networks' history was *Friendster.com*, created in the 2002, that, shaped as a dating site, it focused in helping "friends of friends" meeting. Its success was amazing, and in early January 2004 the growing number of subscriptions was over 5 million (Boyd D. , 2004).

The decline of Friendster involved the problem of "Fakesters", that was the creation of fake profiles, that belonged to fictitious people or not physical persons (such as groups or organizations). The zero tolerance policy of the website against these profiles and their cancellations provoked a lack of trust of the users in the network, which seems constricted in rigid boundaries. At the same time, another social network website was born in Santa Monica, California, with the aim of attract disappointed Friendster users: *MySpace.com*. Launched in August 2003 by Tom Anderson and others, MySpace became the host of rock bands banished from Friendster due to Profiles regulations. Thanks to a highly customizable Profile page, based on the HTML format (the same of websites), bands started to use MySpace as an online platform for reaching fans and promote their music. MySpace keep growing in this niche audience of artists and their fans until the 19 July of 2005, when News Corporation bought Intermix Media (owner of MySpace) for $580 million (BBC, 2005), launching the website into the mainstream attention.

A similar niche approach was used from another social network website: the 4th of February 2004 Harvard student Mark E. Zuckenberg launched a website for helping students to find each other through classes, courses and organizations. He called it "The Facebook" (Phillips S. , 2007). After a mass participation of students of Harvard, Yale and Stanford, in August 2005 *facebook.com* domain was purchased, and it spread in all the educational institutes of the United States. The expansion took a step further in September 2006, when everyone with a registered email address could join the network, establishing the international diffusion of this social network website.

In the last years, the importance of social network website has seen a remarkable growth (Holahan, 2008), which does not seem to stop. In order to analyze this phenomenon there are several dimensions to consider. The worldwide social networks growth, measured by the number of unique visitors, from June 2007 to June 2008 increased of a remarkable 25% (comScore, 2008) against a total internet audience increase of only 11%, proof of a penetration of the social network websites usage; in the United States the growth of social networks is only of 9%, due to a larger visitor base that is closer to the maturation.

Taking into consideration the traffic of websites, *Alexa.com* constantly ranks sites according to the traffic on a daily basis (Alexa) and among the Top 100 most popular websites of the USA per number of visits, *myspace.com* is at the third place and *Facebook.com* at the fifth (September 2008). According to *hitwise.com* instead (HitWise, 2008) in June 2008 among the Top Us domains by traffic, *myspace.com* ranks at the second place, with a market share of 5.05% while *facebook.com* ranks at the ninth place, with a market share of 1.19%.

The analysis can be deepened with the time consumption data: according to *compete.com* (Meattle, 2007), in January 2007 among the Top20 USA domains ranked by attention share, *myspace.com* was at the first place. That means that 11.32% of the total time spent online in the United States was spent on a social network website. *Hitwise.com* (HitWise, 2008) helps to make this data more explicit: a recent report states that the average U.S. time spent for June 2008 on social network websites was 31minutes and 12 seconds for *myspace.com*, 21 minutes and 6 seconds for *facebook.com* and 30 minutes and 31 seconds for *MyYearBook.com* (the third US social network website in the rank by market share). That means that on a sample of 10 million US users, each user spends around half an hour a day on his favourite social network websites.

After this impressive showcase of data, there is no surprise in the increasing spending in online social network advertising: *Emarketer.com* reports (Frank, 2008; eMarketer, 2008) estimate that from 2006 to 2007 the increase was of 163% and from 2007 to 2008 it will be of 55%, with a total amount of spending for the 2008 of $1,430 million, that represents the 5.5% of the total online advertising spending. Beyond the initial excitement, some downsides occurred in establishing which form of advertising works

best in these sites, a challenge that advertisers are still trying to figure out, due to the recent introduction of these platforms.

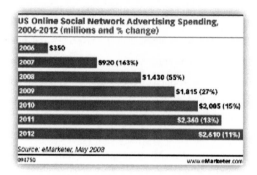

Figure 5 - US Online Social Network Advertising Spending, 2006-2012 (eMarketer, 2008)

In the case of movie marketing, the importance of social networks is even greater that the other industries. Besides spreading the buzz around the film, movie marketers target their efforts to influence the peer-to-peer recommendations (IAB & Microsoft, 2008), that due to the experiential nature of the film, are a strong determination on the decisions of watching a movie. An OTX survey (OTX, 2007) on movie-going behaviour among teens (that are one of the most profitable segments of audience) established that friends' opinions have a major influence on the decision. Since the essence of social network websites are the connections between friends, is clear why the presence of this websites has become a must for all the Studios.

Providing information, spreading the buzz and influencing the recommendations can be all accomplished on social network websites through two types of marketing: *invasive* promotion or *organic* promotion. The *invasive* promotion is described as a *push* type marketing, which is displayed on the user's screen without his approval, usually through the use of banner advertising. There are several strategies to deploy banner ads in social network websites, from the no-brained "carpet bombing" (that is placing ads everywhere and hope to catch the attention of an interested user) to the more advanced targeted ads, like the *Social Ads* introduced by Facebook, that leverage on the interests displayed by users' profiles, trying do deliver ads only to the people that might be interested. Beyond the effectiveness of the last banner ads technologies (that has still to be demonstrated), banner category suffers from a chronic decline of attention of online audience, a phenomenon called *banner blindness*[17] : according to Business Week (BusinessWeek, 2007) in March 2007, the average Click Rate of standard ads banners through the whole Web was of only 0,2%.

The *organic* promotion in social network websites can be instead described as a *pull* marketing tool that aims to model the promoting material on the shape of the platform used. That can be achieved mainly in two ways: creating a Profile and creating a Widget. Referring to Facebook and MySpace as champions of the social networking sites category, in Facebook the Profile assumes the form of the *Page* (that is the equivalent of a profile but designed for Public Figures). Pages usually displays different kind of content embedded in windows pre-established by the Facebook platform, and users can subscribe to the Page becoming *Fans*: in this way every time the Page is updated fans automatically receive a notification; there is also a function for sharing the Page with Facebook friends or display it in the user's Profile. Another Facebook feature that is sometimes used for film promotion is the *Facebook Gifts*: these are small icons that users can send to friends to be displayed on their profile. While regular Gift are usually priced $1, branded gift are offered for free in a limited number.

MySpace lacks of an easy-to-use tool for sharing content with friends, but at the same time it grants to the publisher a complete freedom on the creation of the Profile. All types of HTML content can be easily embedded in the Profile: in this way the layout and all the content of the Profile are under the control of users. Furthermore, while Facebook Pages are created for movies, often in MySpace the promotion of the film is even more organic, with the creation of a Profile for a character of the movie, like a real person. A good example of this strategy is the film *"Borat! Cultural Learnings of America for Make Benefit Glorious Nation of Kazakhstan"*, a comedy mockumentary featuring comedian Sacha Baron Cohen as a reporter of Kazakhstan, produced by Fox. The studio created a

---

[17] The banner blindness is explained in the Widget Marketing paragraph

MySpace profile[18] for the protagonist Borat, and used it to promote the film, reaching a remarkable number of 463,752 friends.

Widgets are instead small applications that can embedded in a website, and in the case of films, they usually displays videos, images and special features, and also the possibility to share it on other pages. Users accept to display a branded widget on their personal Profiles in exchange of an added value to the page, or because they feel passionate about it. While web widgets can be displayed on MySpace profiles like any other websites, it doesn't happen on the Facebook platform, which requires a special widget designed for its environment called "*application*". There are three types of film-promoting applications: they could be simply conversion of an existing widget, they could partner with an existing application for exploiting the existing customer base[19] or they can create a dedicated new application only for Facebook. The first approach is the safest, but will not probably catch the attention of Facebook audience, the third one is the most risky, it could be a success or either a failure while the second one is in the middle, it adds value to the audience but relies to an existing users' base.

3.1 Syndicated content - RSS Feed

RSS (Really Simple Syndication) is the acronym that describes the standard for syndication (Webopedia) of web content, which is the sharing of licensed content among different websites. RSS technology (Webopedia; PCMagazine; Microsoft) is based on a XML format and allows users to subscribe to a RSS feed and then receive any uploaded content directly to their desktop through a RSS reader (that isa software that manage and organize the RSS feeds)

---

[18] http://profile.myspace.com/index.cfm?fuseaction=user.viewprofile&friendid=75796390

[19] See the *30 Days of Night* case in the Widget Marketing paragraph

The RSS format was first developed (RSS Specifications) by Netscape in 1999 for being used on the *mynetscape.com* portal, but the main diffusion on the Web only happened in 2005-2006, when Internet Explorer adopted the RSS orange icon already used in Mozilla Firefox (Microsoft RSS Blog, 2005), promoting in this way the standard for this new information technology. The advantages are considerable both for web publishers and users:

- The publishers (newspapers, bloggers, corporations, products) can reach their audience with uploaded content in a quick and cheap way, feeding the customers with information they are actually interested in (since they voluntarily subscribed).
- Infoseekers can save a tremendous amount of time in the research of information: after an initial investment of time for subscribing to the selected publishers, they automatically receive any new content directly to the RSS feeder, without checking for updates on each website day by day.

Although there are several applications for the RSS technology, the main ones are web blogs and podcasts.

3.2 Syndicated content - Blogs

Blog can be defined as a *"regularly updated journal published on the web"* (Technorati, 2008). Blogs (also called web blogs) are basically pages where any kinds of publishers (from individuals to corporation) post all types of content (text, images, videos, etc.).

Blogs usually have some common features:

27

- Entries are presented in a reverse-chronological order;
- There is the possibility to subscribe to the RSS Feed of the blog, in order to automatically receive any uploaded content without browsing the page;
- Users can (with or without a registration) post their comments to the entries and contribute to the discussion;
- For each topics there are links to other entries or websites, creating a network between blogs talking about the same argument;
- Each entry presents some tags related to the subject (the tags are basically keywords that helps the page to be found when searched);
- Entries are usually classified by date, helping the reader to find old posts;
- Advanced blogs have buttons for sharing the posts in other networks, like Facebook, MySpace, Digg, etc.

The origin of the word "weblog" is probably dated to the 1997, when Jorn Barger (Wortham, 2007) invented the word "weblog" to describe the list of links that he posted on his *Robot Wisdom* website. In the next few years blogs spread widely all over the Internet, creating a *"blogosphere"*, that describes the universe of blogs and their connections in the Web. Technorati, the blog search engine leader of the Internet, has published different reports called "State of the Blogosphere" (Technorati, 2008), stating that the number of blogs tracked through Technorati has grown from 8 millions in the 2005, to 35 millions in the 2006 until the impressive number of 112.8 millions of blogs currently tracked (Technorati, 2008), electing without any doubt the blog as the dominant publishing system of the Internet

Besides private users, in the last years also companies started to acknowledge the power of this new tool (Manjoo, 2002), starting what is called corporate blogging. Companies use blogs to start an open and informal dialogue with their customers, replying to their complaints, feeding them with updated information and maintaining high the level of awareness on the company activities: it is basically a new way to stay in touch with them.

All of this rationale can be fully applied to movie studios and to the releases of new films (Thilk, Movie Marketing and Consumer Control: Part 2, 2006; Thilk, Movie Marketing and Emerging Technology, 2005). First of all the use of film blogs make the audience

28

saving a lot of surfing time: instead of checking through the website new content, the blog could simply summarize day by day every new upload, from downloads to new clips. Moreover, production blogs for example stimulate the interest of audience with constant uploads on the status of an upcoming film, keeping high the awareness about the movie and helping to spread the buzz around it. Besides, a side-effect is the sense of involvement that the audience start to feel about the film, creating the compelling experience of watching day by day the film evolving from a script to a final cut, stimulating a dialogue between the filmmaker and his audience. If regularly updated with new entries and receives a lot of comments and links, blogs can be easily be found on the top ranking in the organic search results pages of search engines, an extremely important goal[20].

The first Studio that embraced blogs to promote films is Sony (Thilk, Movie Marketing and Consumer Control: Part 3, 2006), with the production blog for *Spiderman 2* in 2004[21]. It was written by Grant Curtis, co-producer of Spiderman trilogy, and followed the production from the very early stages (the location scouting) to the very end (the release of the DVD for the Home Video), allowing also fans to comment each post and then receive the reply from the co-producer. Even more effective are the production blogs directly updated by the directors of films, a fact that greatly amplify the effectiveness of this tool. One of the most famous examples (Lee, 2005; Thilk, Movie Marketing and Consumer Control: Part 3, 2006) are the video production blog[22] of Peter Jackson during his remake of *King Kong* in 2005 and the weekly video diary of *Superman Returns'* director Bryan Singer[23]. Singer strongly supported the blog, declaring *"If you're willing to expose yourself a bit, it can be a wonderful method of getting the word out and sharing that experience with the people who are most interested -- the fans"*, at the opposite of movies official websites, that are tagged as *"a bit stagnant"* and *"so traditional"*. And according to the statistics his vision is right: Peter Jackson's diary received 100,000 downloads a week while Bryan's blog was viewed about 50,000 times a day.

---

[20] See the Search Engine Marketing paragraph.

[21] http://spiderman.sonypictures.com/movies/spiderman2/productionblog/

[22] http://www.kongisking.net

[23] http://www.bluetights.net

The opportunity of receiving film updates directly from the directors is unique and extremely powerful, and studios start to recognize it. Fox Searchlight Pictures (Thilk, Movie Marketing and Consumer Control: Part 3, 2006), for example, besides having its own corporate blog, promoted different directors' blogs, like the one of Jason Reitman for *Thank you for smoking* and for the Zach Braff's *Garden State*. Another great example of the work of this innovative studio is the Danny Boyle's film *Sunshine*, which published a blog about the film for over two years: this created a strong community around a niche film (IAB & Microsoft, 2008), achieving also the hard goal (due to the extremely common word) of placing the website on the top of the search engine pages results.

Figure 7 - Sunshine's Movie Blog

Blogs definitely represents the most important medium for publishing content in the Internet. Film blogs if wisely used can be a one-stop point in providing updated information to movie infoseekers and also an effective way for creating involvement in the audience. They also contribute to generate a level of awareness around films that could help to spread the buzz, creating in this way a sort of loyal customer base that will follow films' development until the theatrical release and also beyond.

Podcast is an internet technology based on RSS Feed that allows users to automatically download content from a publishing websites they subscribed to into their personal devices, usually portable MP3 players or PC. The word Podcast was created by the former MTV *VJ* Adam Curry combining the word broadcasting (that is the distribution of content) and the word iPod, the Apple's most popular MP3 player, for describing a technology to push content from websites to the portable players (Podcast Alley; PC Magazine; Oxford University Press; Van Orden).

Podcast is a very simple way to consume content: users browse websites and once they found an interesting broadcasted content they can subscribe to its RSS Feed, and every time they connect their portable device any updated content is automatically downloaded and installed in the player. Podcast can be also used on computers, without having necessarily a portable player device.

Usually the content is audio (audio podcasts) or video (video podcasts). Podcast subscriptions and downloads are managed through a podcast aggregator or podcatcher, that checks on Internet for any updated content and automatically download it. One of the most widespread podcatcher and podcast platforms is the Apple iTunes, that besides being a virtual shop for music and video, it provides also a deep selection of audio and video podcast usually for free.

Hollywood studios have just started to create video podcasts (Thilk, Movie Marketing and Emerging Technology, 2005): on iTunes is Disney that is the most represented studios, with a general video podcasts for new trailers and some dedicated ones for specific film content, like the Pixar animated *Cars* or the adventure flick *Pirates of the Caribbean* (implemented by the UK division). The content broadcasted by film podcast may vary from trailers and TV clips to "behind the scenes" videos, like the podcast created by Warner Bros about the making of the epic film *300*. An interesting use of video podcasts for marketing an upcoming film was the *Bryan's Journals*, where director Bryan Singer tell to the audience about making *Superman Returns* through short videos, with a total collection of 30 entries

Besides the type of content, one of the most important quality of a podcast is the frequency of new updates: subscribing to a podcast means a willingness of the user to periodically receive new content, so creating a podcast for just a couple of trailers and clips is not a proper use of this powerful marketing tool. More frequent content means a superior level of engagement of the audience, reached through an additional media, which are the portable players.

4. Mobile Marketing

Mobile is often indicated by marketers as the new medium that soon will take a consistent stake in the total advertising spending pie: from the last year, the worldwide advertising spending has seen an impressive growth that seems to increase exponentially in the next years:

Mobile Advertising Spending Worldwide, by Format, 2007-2012 (millions)						
	2007	2008	2009	2010	2011	2012
Mobile message advertising*	$2,560	$4,200	$6,440	$9,260	$11,960	$14,173
Mobile display advertising**	$52	$142	$338	$629	$945	$1,203
Mobile search advertising***	$83	$244	$597	$1,290	$2,345	$3,773
Total	$2,695	$4,586	$7,375	$11,179	$15,250	$19,149

Note: numbers may not add up to total due to rounding; *spending on placement in text messages, includes direct spending on message campaigns as well as spending on promotional coverage of end-user messaging costs; **spending on display banners, links or icons placed on WAP, mobile HTML sites or embedded in mobile applications such as maps or entertainment services (e.g. games or video); ***spending on sponsored display ads and text links that appear alongside mobile search results, as well as spending on audio ads played to mobile phone callers making a directory inquiry
Source: eMarketer, March 2008

092628   www.eMarketer.com

Figure 8 - Mobile Advertising Spending Worldwide, by Format, 2007-2012

Of this spending, only in the US market the investment will raise from the $1.7 billion in the 2008 to $6.5 billion in the 2012. This trust of the market towards the mobile market has different explanations.

From a statistic perspective the situation of the mobile market is more than cheering. According to CTIA[24] at the end of 2007 the number of US mobile subscribers was of 254 million of user (Nielsen, 2008) that is around the 84% of the US population: SNL KAGAN estimates that the subscribers' number will grow yearly by 3%, reaching a 100% penetration of the US market by 2013 (SNLKagan, 2007).

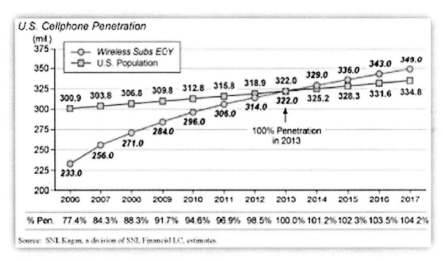

Figure 9 - U.S. Cellphone Penetration (SNLKagan, 2007)

Beyond message advertising that uses SMS (text) and MMS (images, videos) to deliver the promotional message directly to the display of the user's phone, all mobile marketing is based on mobile internet, that is the access to the Web through mobiles. The recent report *"Critical Mass: the worldwide state of the Mobile Web"* released by Nielsen states:

- *"95 million (37 percent) US mobile subscribers paid for access to the mobile Internet, either as part of a subscription or transactionally;*
- *40 million subscribers (15.6 percent in May 2008) were active users of mobile Internet services, using those services at least once on a monthly basis;*

---

[24] It's the U.S. wireless industry trade group, http://www.ctia.org.

- *the number of monthly unique users of the mobile Internet increased 73 percent from May 2006 (23.4 million) to May 2008 (40.4 million)."* (Nielsen, 2008)

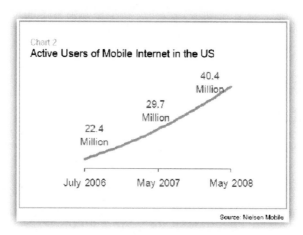

Figure 10 - Active Users of Mobile Internet in the US (Nielsen, 2008)

Moreover, according to MPAA media consumption statistics (MPAA, 2008), between 2006 and 2007 the consumption per hours per person of mobile content has increased by 38.5%, that is the biggest increase in all media category. With 40 million of active users, mobile internet has become a mass medium with a steady yearly growth, representing an attractive target for mobile marketing strategies.

Marketers can deploy different tools to address mobile consumers (Nichols, 2008; Bourke, 2006):

- mobile websites: brands should design a version of their websites to facilitate the mobile internet navigation. That means a simpler layout, less graphics and more text, for reasons of screen size (the navigation on a small mobile's screen is completely different than a computer) and also of bandwidth load (complex pages will take too much time to download and display on the mobiles);
- message advertising: promotional messages (text or multimedia ones) can be sent directly to users' mobiles, offering coupons or information about new prod-

ucts. It is important that addressed users have previously accepted to be listed for advertising, otherwise is prohibited.

- mobile search advertising: it works in the same way of the internet one, with the difference that being on top of searches is more important in mobiles. Ads are priced on a pay per click basis;
- advertising banners: they can be purchases on portals (websites provided by the Mobile company to access the mobile internet) or on external websites;
- downloadable content: brands can offers users wallpapers, screensavers or ring-tones to customize their mobiles with branded material;
- mobile games or applications: mobile gamers are expected to grow from 406 million in 2007 to 596 million in 2009 (eMarketer, 2008) and as in December 2007 players were 21% (comScore, 2008) of the total U.S. mobile subscribers. Games are indeed a powerful tool to create awareness around a brand: gamers are more inclined to play advertised games for free instead of paying for downloading ad-free ones, creating a huge opportunity for brands that want to target the gamers segment of populations (Nichols, 2008).

The use of mobile marketing is growing at a fast pace: Nielsen estimates that at the end of 2007 29% of US mobile subscribers have seen a form of advertising in the previous 30 days and around half of the mobile data subscribers responded in some way to an ad displayed on the phone (Walsh, Nielsen: Improved Recall, Comfort With Mobile Ads, 2008). The receptiveness of mobile audience is therefore higher than other audiences, but at the same time the marketing strategy should carefully consider the personal and private nature of this medium, correctly balancing the violation of the privacy with the benefits offered as extra value by the promotion.

Like any other industry, also film industry started to include mobiles in their marketing media planning, utilizing a range of tools that vary from standard messaging advertising to creative cross media campaigns: for the promotion of the comedy *Forgetting Sarah Marshalls* Universal Pictures partnered with 4INFO ad network to target a selected audience of 18-34 males with promotional messages about the movie (Mobile Marketing Association, 2008). They delivered messages with film information, a mobile trailer and links to the website, accomplishing an increase in the brand awareness of 19.7%. A simi-

35

lar result is achieved with the viral phone messages[25]: for the promotion of the New Line Cinema thriller *Snakes on a Plane*, users could go on the official website and insert the phone number of a friend and some details of his life. The result was a phone call with the voice of Samuel L. Jackson (star of the movie) urging to go to watch his new released film (Leo, 2006).

The most standard mobile marketing tools is anyway a package of content such as wallpapers or ringtones that users can download from the mobile Web page of the film, the official website or the website of a third-party that partners with the Studio releasing the film; the same happens with mobile games, that often are released with the film. A good example of this strategy happened with the release of *The Simpsons: The movie*, when Fox partnered with the mobile content provider Jamster to create a one-stop portal for all The Simpsons branded mobile content, providing also a monthly subscription *yellow plan*[26] (Thilk, Movie Marketing Madness: The Simpsons Movie, 2007). That represents a unique way to build awareness on the brand and at the same time leveraging on it for earning an extra profit.

5.1 Advergaming

Advergaming is a form of marketing that uses videogames to promote a brand or a product. The rationale behind the use of advergaming is to overcome the resistance of audience towards explicit advertising through the offering of an extra value, which is the entertainment of playing the game. Audience gets in touch with the brand not through a passive exposure like standard advertising (like billboards or TV commercials), but through an active interaction with the branded content, increasing and setting a more persistent brand awareness.

The term advergaming was probably coined in 2000 by Anthony Giallourakis, which purchased the domain *advergames.com* (Obringer; Loewenhagen). One of the first men-

---

[25] See "Viral Marketing: Viral Messages" paragraph.

[26] http://www.thesimpsonsmobile.com

tion was anyway in the Wired Magazine's "Jargon Watch" column, where it was used to described the online games available on the Web that have been commissioned by brands or products.

There are several ways to use videogames for marketing purposes, but it is possible to identify four main categories (Buckner, Fang, & Quiao, 2002; Chen & Ringel, 2001):

1. Online promotional games: these are Internet-based games where the brand or product content is clearly visible, if not protagonist of the game itself. They are usually based on Flash technology (that is a standard for designing and delivering content supporter by all web browsers), embedded inside website pages or in social network websites (like for example the Facebook Applications) and are provide usually a simple gameplay (arcade or puzzle). Best games offer an experience that is very tight to the plot of the movie. Besides attract and keep audience on the website, online games could trigger a viral effect: if the player judges the game experience very entertaining he will share it with his friends, spreading in this way brand awareness.

2. Branded videogames: these are complete videogames that are published on platforms like consoles or PC, where the gameplay usually involve the brand content. This is the case of the videogames based on sport associations (like FIFA or Formula 1) or films franchises. Another example is placing the product or the brand as an integrated part of the gameplay: for example in the Electronic Arts *NASCAR 06: Total Team Control* players can race with a UPS truck, a strategy that could be assimilated to film product placement (UPS, 2005).

3. In-game advertising: this is the placement of advertising banners inside the gameplay, usually through virtual billboards or virtual props of the product (like for example Pepsi's vendor machines inside first-person action games). While other forms of interruptive advertising are received with indifference by audience, in-game advertising seems to have a positive effect on the gameplay, and according to a study conducted by Nielsen BASES and Nielsen Games on behalf of in-game advertising network IGA Worldwide, over 60% of the players surveyed had positive opinions towards this new innovative form of brand promotion (Nielsen Games, 2008).

Figure 11 - Example of In-Game Advertising (Cavalli, 2008)

4. Alternative Reality Game: ARGs are advanced interactive games that cross several media (so they are not only online) for setting a deep experience for the audience. Even if basically are games that can be used for promotional purposes, ARGs are at the boundaries of the advergaming category, and they deserve a dedicated analysis.

Of these categories, the preferred Advergaming by Hollywood is beyond doubts the online games: in film official websites is always more frequent to find various types of flash games, which try to improve the site's surfing experience and entertain the audience. Besides being on official websites, some games are offered in other platforms, such as social networks websites (like Facebook) or dedicated mini-websites for the more complex games. The fact the nowadays almost all the official websites have some kind of flash games, make more difficult for a game to be remarkable: engaging gameplay and deep use of the film content may be some winning factors.

Film-based videogames have always been a successful franchise, since the born of the videogames industry in the '80s. For an upcoming movie, the release of the related videogame may represent an additional boost of awareness (and revenues, if the videogame is successful). At the opposite, in-game advertising is still to be fully exploited by film marketers: problems may arise trying to match the timeline of the film and the videogame production. Videogames, like films, needs up to 4 years to be developed, and marketers need to find a videogame which release is close to the film's one, a matching that is not easy to accomplish. A great example of a recent in-game advertising is for the Ben Stiller action comedy *Tropic Thunder*, that named an homonymous campaign in the videogame *"Tom Clancy's Rainbow Six: Vegas2"*, that after be completed by the players unlock exclusive content about the film (Radd, 2008).

The benefits of advergaming for movie marketers should grow expectations for an increased use of this marketing tool in the next years: first of all advertising within engaging game experiences has been reported to have a strong positive impact on audience (Beirne, 2008). A study conducted by Nielsen (Nielsen Entertainment, 2007) reported that in-game ads, for example, have a strong impact in increasing brand familiarity, brand rating, ad rating and recall: audience simply likes this kind of advertising. Besides a high effectiveness, advergaming matches with movie marketing also for its range: videogames' demographics researches states that the segment of population with the highest videogame penetration is the 18-34 male segment (67.7%), that is also the segment of frequent moviegoers (ESA, 2008; MPAA, 2008). This means that through advergaming, studios can reach their priority audience through an effective and "welcomed" type of advertising, with better results in awareness and buzz-generation.

5.2 Alternative Reality Game

The Alternative Reality Game is a concept that is not easy to define. If technically belongs to the family of Massively Multiplayer Online Game, an ARG has features completely different. An ARG does not require any installed software to play, it is not played only online but it crosses a broad range of media and above all *"is not a game"*, that is the principle on whom is build an ARG. Actually the very particularity of this kind of interactive fiction is that the player is not entering the game's world, but it is the game that enters in the player's world, integrating in his real life of every day (Borland, 2005)

Probably one of the best representations of an Alternative Reality Game is the David Fincher's film *The Game*, where Michael Douglas plays an investment banker that for his birthday receives from his brother the participation in a game that will change his life forever (IGDA, 2006). Anyway, an exhaustive definition of an ARG is the one provided on the ARG dedicated website *unfiction.com*[27]:

"Alternate Reality Gaming [...] is an interactive fusion of creative writing, puzzle-solving, and team-building, with a dose of role playing thrown in. It utilizes several forms of media in order to pass clues to the players, who solve puzzles in order to win pieces of the story being played out. Clues can be passed through web pages, email, voicemail, snail mail, television advertisements, movie posters, campus billboards, newspaper classifieds... really, in any way that information can be passed. [...]. This genre of game almost requires participation in a group or community that works together to win past the more difficult hurdles."

In film industry, the precursor of the modern ARGs was the campaign behind *The Blair Witched Project* in 1999, that, mixing elements of viral marketing and ARG, engaged the online audience in a parallel world in order to give authenticity to the story and make appear real the mockumentary about the disappeared actors (IGDA, 2006).

The first recognized ARG that defined the standards for this genre was created in 2001 for the promotion of the Steven Spielberg film *Artificial Intelligence*: ideated by a team leaded by Jordan Weisman and Elan Lee, both Microsoft's employees, it was called *The Beast*, since the number of items of the early project was 666 (Handy, 2005). The game started on April 11 with the first clue hidden in a fictitious credit on the official movie poster and it ended on July 24[28] 2001 involving in just three months more than 3 million players around the world[29], with several web communities of thousands of players that cooperated to solve the game (like the Cloudmakers, the most famous group that solved the game) (Hon, 2005)

The Beast contributed to define the basic design principles that usually all the ARGs have (Saleem, 2007; Stewart, 2006):

---

[27] http://www.unfiction.com/glossary/

[28] http://cloudmakers.org/

[29] http://42entertainment.com

- Interactive and Fragmented Narrative: a compelling story is probably the most important element of an ARG. The designers have to create a complete background reality for the game and also make it dynamic, since the sequence of events should develop according to the (re)actions of the players, in a sort of collaborative growth of the narration. Usually the pieces of the story are scattered through different media and in a non-chronological order;
- Social Games: challenges usually are in finding clues, hidden through different media, and decipher them, in order to find the next ones. Anyway the difficult of puzzles push players to collaborate together, fostering the creation of web communities which members cooperate actively to find and share the clues and solve the game. The social effect during the adventure is one of the strengths of ARGs.
- Cross-media development: the use of multiple media contributes to increase the broadness and deepness of the ARG. Each medium is preferred by a different segment of the population, and making the game accessible from many different platforms allows the broadening of the audience. Moreover, an ARG that spans through a lot of media acquire a stronger tone of realism and legitimation: if the game has to enter in the player's world it has to integrate with the great number of media that characterize that world, such as Internet (with the all range of online tools, from blog to chat to podcasts and so on), telephone, television, newspapers, billboards, radio, etc.
- This Is Not A Game look (McGonigal, 2003): the principle is simple, the game does not have to admit to be a game! The appeal of be involved in an ARG is in thinking that what is happening is real, even if obviously it is not (*The Beast* story, for example, was dated in year 2142). That is why there should not be explicit rules for playing, and all the material has to be existing (mentioned websites, phone numbers, places to go, etc.): the experience happens only once, and in real time, involving real people.

Basically we can distinguish two types of ARGs, the ones with a promotional purpose and those without. The ARGs without a promotional purpose are usually created by fans for the pure entertainment of the players. Despite the high risk of failure of this games, like the lack of funding and a volunteer workforce, in the last few years non promotional

ARGs has gained the largest share, thanks to an established community of fans and a steady demand for this kind of entertainment.

The origins of the ARGs are anyway as promotional. *The Beast* was created to promote the film *Artificial Intelligence*, *I Love Bees* for the Microsoft videogame Halo2, *Year Zero* for the upcoming release of the new album of the rock band *Nine Inch Nails* (Rose, 2007), *The Lost Experience* for the promotion of the ABC TV show *Lost*: the history of ARGs is dominated by this high profile projects, that thanks to a strong corporate support and a worldwide media coverage, are usually referred to define the genre.

From a marketing perspective (Hamburg, 2008; Colantonio; Carton, 2005), the ARGs can be classified as part buzz marketing, part viral marketing and part experiential marketing. ARGs are buzz marketing tools because they reach a very broad audience through a wide variety of media, creating a cross-media buzz that, besides involving the players of the game, provoke an impressive media coverage. ARGs can be viewed instead as viral marketing campaigns due to the creation of a creative content (basically the game per se) that is extremely appealing for the user\player, that becomes passionate about it, sharing it with other people, especially online. ARGs can be also subscribed to the category of Experience Marketing (Pine II & Gilmore, 1999), since their essence is exactly in setting a valuable experience through a strong involvement of the customer (aka player), in the effort to excite commitment and passion about the brand or its values: players of *The Lost Experience* probably liked the ABC's TV show also before the ARG, nevertheless this effort was aimed to strengthen (and broaden) the customer base of *Lost*, and obviously spread the buzz.

It is important to stress that Alternative Reality Games are not just marketing tools, but they are more similar to a form of entertainment, even if they can be used for marketing purposes. Just like brands promote in films through product placement, or in music events through sponsorships, ARGs can be used as a vehicle for creating awareness on a brand\product, spreading a buzz around it that is going to catch the media attention. But while the audience watch a film in theatres or listen to a music concert, in ARGs the audience PLAYS the adventure, and interaction is the key; that's why the effectiveness of these games relies in the total engagement of the player.

The benefits for a brand in implementing an ARG to promote a product launch are beyond dispute (Dena, 2008): the *I Love Bees* ARG for the promotion of the videogame *Halo2* resulted in $125 million in copies sold in the first day of release, and it is part of the Hollywood history the success of *The Blair Witch Project* (a marketing budget of about $1.5 million with a worldwide gross result of over $240 millions[30]). There are anyway downsides that the brand should carefully considers: besides the costs of realizing an ARG and the risk of a low participation of audience, the main problem is that the success of the game does not equalize the success of the brand\product associated. The proof of this actual lack of correlation between the ARG success and the brand\product sales is the most famous and successful ARG: *The Beast*. It attracted over 3 million of players, but the film *Artificial Intelligence* (with a production budget of $100 millions[31]) resulted in a domestic box office gross of only $78 million[32] avoiding a complete flop only with the world wide release.

6. Cross Brand Promotion

Films and brands have always had a kind of synergy. Films need brands as sponsors and brands look for advertising in films, a strong relationship that comes from both the parts (Dennis, 2008). From the Hollywood side, the motivation can be easily found in the increasing cost of producing and especially marketing a film. The production budget of a Hollywood film is becoming bigger year after year, and due to this heavy investment is well understandable that studios want to reduce the risk of a box office flop. The first solution is allocating more and more money to the marketing campaign of the film, focusing all the efforts (and the money) to raise awareness around the release through advertising on a range of media that is way wider than a couple of decades ago: TV, radio, newspapers, billboards, internet, mobile and so on.

---

[30] http://imdb.com

[31] http://boxofficemojo.com

[32] http://boxofficemojo.com

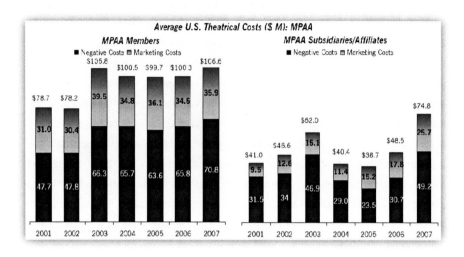

Figure 12 - Average U.S. Theatrical Costs (MPAA, 2008)

Basically brands can help studios to finance the marketing expenses of launching a new film, providing the additional resources needed to implement a successful marketing campaign. But it is not only a mere matter of money.

Recently, the historical relationship between films and brands has seen a radical shift from a quantity to a quality approach (Brodesser-Akner, 2008). For film promotion, a quantity approach means having as many sponsors as possible, in order to collect the biggest possible amount of capital to cover marketing expenses. An example of this cross brand promotion strategy is the James Bond film franchise: for *Die Another Day* MGM studios spent $30 million in advertising, but raised more than $120 million from more than 20 brand promoting partners (Magzan, 2002). And for *Tomorrow Never Dies* the capital collected reached the record amount of $160 million. Despite a good box office results, these films have been criticised to be nothing else than long commercials (The Hollywood Reporter, 2005)

Figure 13 - The over-advertised James Bond franchise

The quality approach, as suggested by the Paramount's senior VP-worldwide marketing partnerships Lee Anne Stables (Brodesser-Akner, 2008) consists in *"the shortest list of partners with the biggest impact"*, that grants studios to focus on a small number of partnership deals, with considerable savings of efforts and time. The process of selection of the ideal partners consists in:

1. List all the possible *"hooks"* of the film (the hook is a factor of attractiveness towards a specific segment of audience) and identify one or more segments of audience for each hook.
2. Identify for each segment of audience the brand that can reach in the most effective way the selected target.

The key word of the overall cross branding marketing strategy has to be consistency. Consistency between the hook and the brand selected, between the hook's audience and the brand's audience and between the different promotions implemented by each partner and the core values of the film.

From the brands' side, the Hollywood history is full of examples on how a film could change the destiny of a brand, due to the cultural and social impact that films has on the audience. One of the first films that showed this influence was in 1934, where in a *"It Happened One Night"* scene Clark Cable, while he was undressing before going to sleep,

45

was seen without undershirt: after the film's release in theatres the sales of men's undershirt dropped of 75% (The Hollywood Reporter, 2005). Even if probably the film was not the only cause of the sales' decline, the fact of showing in a film the preferences of a cultural icon such as Clark Cable had a strong influence on the shopping attitudes of male audience (Gottschalk, 1995). A side effect of that film and others released in the following decades was the implementation of another form of advertising partnerships between brands and film: the product placement.

The product placement in film is a form of advertising that consists in showing a product or a brand inside a film (Dalli, 2003; Gutnik, Huang, Blue Lin, & Schmidt, 2007). The product can be simply shown on the screen, used by a character or placed on the background (screen placement), the product\brand can be mentioned in a dialogue (script placement) or it can be integrated in the story (plot placement). In exchange of the placement, the brand can provide the products to be used in the film production for free (like the placement of cars or locations) or pay a fee or both. Product placement and Cross Brand Promotion are two different strategies, but it is frequent for brands to implement a cross brand promotional deal as a following to product placement (Sauer, 2005), in order to strengthen the association between brand and film and maintaining high the level of awareness. This is especially frequent for small brands that would be hardly recognized through a simple product placement.

For the brands than can not benefit of a direct presence in the film, being a promotional partner of the film is the only strategy that could be implemented. Like in a product placement deal, the duty for the brand could be paying a fee for associating the film with the brand in the promotional material or grant to the Studio a marketing coverage to support the promotion of the film or a combination of the two. Usually the online tools used by partners are dedicated mini websites, contests, sweepstakes and User Generated Content initiatives, even if almost all the online marketing tools can be utilized by partners for film promotion. For example, Sony Pictures dealt with Google for the launch of *The Da Vinci Code*: users have to download a *"Da Vinci Code Quest on Google"* module on their homepage and each day try to solve a puzzle using different tools of Google, like Google Maps, Google Video and Google SMS, with a final prize for the winner. In that month of promotion, the visit to Sony and Google websites simply skyrocketed, and the movie revenues were over $758[33] million worldwide (Lenssen, 2006).

Figure 14 - The Da Vinci Code on Google

Another example is the collaboration between MGM and eBay for the launch of *Rocky Balboa*, the last episode of the Sylvester Stallone franchise released on December 2007. They posted the actor's voice on the eBay homepage with the film's catchphrase "*It ain't over 'til it's over*", promoting the sale of movie memorabilia and, much more important, a campaign of direct e-mails to eBay customers, that during the Christmas period reach a peak of over 75 million of people. While eBay added valuable content to its website, MGM bridged the gap between old fans of rocky movies and a broader audience (Stanley, 2006).

The advantages for a brand to be the promotional partner of a film are various: first of all the buzz generated by the film marketing campaign indirectly affects the sponsor brand. Also using the film content (like the characters or also the actors) represents an effective way to differentiate the product and stand above the competitors. Finally for some brands (like cars or luxury products) cross brand promotions can be used to set in the mind of audience a defined brand value, exploiting the values of the film. For example, Jeep partnered with Paramount Pictures for the adventure films *"Tomb Raider: Cradle of Life"* and *"Sahara"* placing Jeep vehicles (Product Placement) in the films and contributing substantially to the marketing campaign with an extended advertising and publicity campaign. The goal was to strengthen the "adventure" and "fun" factors of the Jeep brand partnering with films that share the same values (The Auto Channel, 2005)

---

[33] http://www.boxofficemojo.com

7.1. Viral Marketing - Introduction to the concepts

Viral marketing is one of the most recent ways used by Hollywood studios to promote films through the Internet. The power of this tool was unleashed in the 1999 with the marketing campaign for *The Blair Witch Project*, a low-budget horror movie that for the first time targeted the online audience with viral marketing tools, obtaining an outstanding success. But what is the definition of viral marketing? And what is the difference between viral, buzz and word of mouth marketing?

The term *Viral Marketing* was first introduced in the 1996 by the Harvard professor Jeffrey Rayport in the article *The Virus of Marketing* (Rayport, 1996), where he explained this new approach to marketing through analogies with viruses. Nevertheless, the viral marketing came to the mainstream attention only with the astonishing success of the Hotmail viral campaign, created in the 1997 by Steve Jurvetson and Tim Draper, the Hotmail's venture capitalists (Jurvetson & Draper, 2001) that defined viral marketing as *"a type of marketing that infects its customers with an advertising message, which passes from one customer to the next like a rampant flu virus"* (Montgomery, 2001, p. 93).

There are dozens of definitions of viral marketing that consider different aspects and faces of it, but almost all of them are characterized by two core elements:

- a marketing message disguised in a compelling creative content, which leverages on the interests of the customers, making him feel so passionate about that he is willing to invest his time and reputation to...
- spread and share the content\message with other people, above all through the Internet, like blogs, social networks, emails, discussion forums and so on.

Marketing experts agree that viral marketing, buzz marketing and word of mouth are all different concepts, even if the boundary of each definition may differ from researcher to researcher. Marketing guru Seth Godin on his homonymous blog[34] argues that *"Word of mouth is a decaying function. A marketer does something and a consumer tells five or ten*

---

[34] http://sethgodin.typepad.com/

friends. And that's it. It amplifies the marketing action and then fades, usually quickly" (Godin, Is viral marketing the same as word of mouth?, 2007)

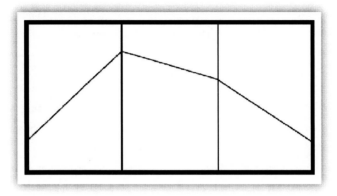

"Here's a schematic of typical word of mouth. Notice how few cycles there are, and how it drops off over time." (Godin, Unleashing the Ideavirus, 2000, p. 32)

Figure 15- Word of mouth as a decaying function

While *"Viral marketing is a compounding function. A marketer does something and then a consumer tells five or ten people. Then they tell five or ten people. And it repeats. And grows and grows. Like a virus spreading through a population"* (Godin, Is viral marketing the same as word of mouth?, 2007).

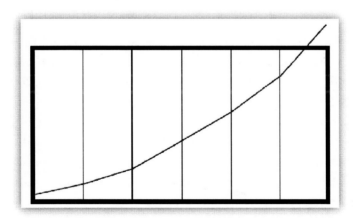

"Here's an ideal ideavirus. Note how much more frequently the cycles occur, and how each cycle sees the virus grow." (Godin, Unleashing the Ideavirus, 2000, p. 32)

Figure 16 - Viral marketing is a compounding function

From his point of view, Viral Marketing is a kind of evolution of the WOM marketing on two different levels: the first one is the message, which is designed to appeal to the interests of the customer, making him feel intimate with that. The second one is the media used: the Internet is the optimal environment where the Viral message (what Seth Godin in his book define also as *ideavirus*) can easily grow and spread from customer to customer, without any further effort of the marketer.

Slightly different is the vision presented by Dave Balter and John Butman in the book *Grapevine*, where *"buzz is a marketing tactic aimed at generating publicity or awareness often without regard to any specific message, while Viral Marketing is a mean of spreading a marketing message through the use of a contagious creative most often Web-video and Word Of Mouth is the process of product story-telling"* (Bader; Balter, 2008)

The output of the two marketing strategies is totally different: the Buzz Marketing will focus his efforts on the creation of an "event" attractive enough to make people talk about it to other people via Word Of Mouth. Viral Marketing is instead the creation of a message that deeply appeals to a specific segment of customers that will carry the virus "infecting" other people, via Word Of Mouth or more likely via its online version *Word Of Mouse*, since happens that Viral Marketing develops and spreads more easily through the Internet.

About the Word Of Mouth (Word of Mouth Marketing Association, 2006) is interesting to point out a distinction suggested by Glenn Gabe (Gabe, The Difference Between Bzz Marketing, Viral Marketing, and Word of Mouth Marketing, 2006; Gabe, So Now It's Called WOM!, 2006) and others. WOM could be *organic* or *induced*. The organic WOM is when a customer genuinely talks to another customer about a product or his experience with a product, providing him information, and it naturally happens everyday. On the internet, surfers talk about their experiences in blogs, discussion forums, social networks, reaching an extremely broad audience in a short time, making the Word Of Mouse an extremely powerful force that companies should carefully monitor. For example, if a user has just seen the last Spielberg's flick and loved it, he's probably going to write a positive review on his blog, or post a comment in his Facebook profile or send an email to his friends, trigging a chain reaction.

The induced WOM is instead the result of a marketing effort aimed to create awareness around a brand or a product, obtained for example through a Buzz Marketing campaign or also a Viral one. For example, before the release of a Spielberg's film, studio releases a video on YouTube where the famous director jokes with the actors about something happened during the production of the film or there is a press release about a fight happened between two actors casting in the movie. This is all created to spread the buzz around the upcoming film, giving the surfers something to talk about, triggering the conversation.

In order to proceed with the application of these tools to the online marketing of films, it is possible to assume that:

- the Word Of Mouth is simply the action of talking about something; the environment of analysis is the Internet so the WOM is considered as Word Of Mouse and, since it is a consequent of marketing efforts, is an induced WOM;
- to be considered Buzz Marketing a tool has to be under the form of an event or a news created online or offline by the marketing team , and has to be able to rise interest and make people talk about it via WOM;
- the Viral Marketing is instead characterized by a compelling online content (video, audio, image, etc.) containing a marketing message that is able to increasingly spread from user to user exploiting the WOM.

7.2 Viral Marketing - Viral Messages

An online marketing tool that is recently used in a large number of film promoting campaigns is the viral message, which is created through an online interactive platform with the participation of the user. The specific goal is inviting the user in the creation of a creative message related to the film and convincing him to share it with friends, spreading and increasing the film awareness through word of mouth (or better word of mouse).

The elements of viral messages can be summarized in:

1. An online interactive platform: it is basically the application for creating the message, and it can be placed on the official website of the film, on a dedicated microsite, inside a social network (like a Facebook Application) or through a mobile application (like the *The Dark Knight: HaHaHa* application for the iPhone created for the promotion of *The Dark Knight*). The simultaneous presence of the platform in more places helps to reach a broader audience;

Figure 17 - The Dark Knight's iPhone Application

2. The participation of the user: for example is asked to the user to upload a photo that will be embedded in the output or to actively create the message with tools provided by the platform. For the promotion of *The 40-Year-Old Virgin* Universal created *Make a man-o-lantern*, where user could type a message that will appear in the ripped-off chest hair of Steve Carrel (Thilk, Movie Marketing and Consumer Control: Part 3, 2006);
3. The sharing of the message: once the process of creating the message is finished, the platform encourages the user to share the output with friend(s), in order to trigger the viral effect; usually it's shared through email, social network profiles or mobile phones. For example, for the DVD release of the horror flick *The Ring 2*

on the website *7daysleft.com* users could enter the email addresses and phone numbers of up to six friends: these friends then received an email containing the scary video from the film and, and when it was ended they received a mysterious phone call stating they had seven days left to live (Nudd, 2005).

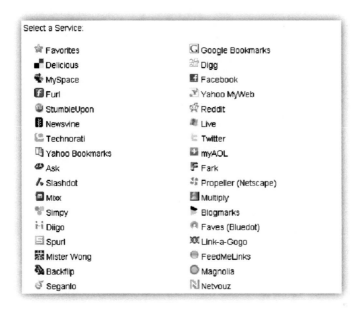

Figure 18 · An example of different sharing platforms

8. Search Engine Marketing

The category of search engine marketing includes all the techniques aimed to increase the visibility of a website in the search engine results pages (SEMPO, 2008). Among the others tool, SEM is actually the type of online advertising that receives the biggest investments, a trend that is going to continue in the next years. The popularity of SEM is due to its nature of non-interruption advertising. Usually standard advertising tries to catch the attention of audience while it is doing something: TV commercials while watching a film, billboards while driving in the traffic, ad banners while surfing the Web, these are all examples of advertising that interrupt the audience. In the case of SEM instead, the user is performing a research on search engines because he is actually looking for information and advertising will provide him exactly what he is looking for, shifting from an annoying interruption to a useful value provider.

US Online Advertising Spending, by Format, 2006-2011 (millions)						
	2006	2007	2008	2009	2010	2011
Search	$6,799	$8,624	$11,000	$12,935	$14,906	$16,590
Display ads	$3,685	$4,687	$5,913	$6,663	$7,500	$8,190
Classified	$3,059	$3,638	$4,675	$5,493	$6,281	$6,930
Rich media/video	$1,192	$1,755	$2,613	$3,575	$4,463	$5,481
Lead generation*	$1,310	$1,733	$2,269	$2,795	$3,281	$3,675
E-Mail	$338	$428	$481	$553	$600	$630
Sponsorships	$496	$535	$550	$488	$469	$504
Total	**$16,879**	**$21,400**	**$27,500**	**$32,500**	**$37,500**	**$42,000**

Note: eMarketer benchmarks its US online advertising spending projections against the Interactive Advertising Bureau (IAB)/PricewaterhouseCoopers (PwC) data, for which the last full year measured was 2006; online ad data includes categories as defined by IAB/PWC benchmark—display ads (such as banners), search ads (including paid listings, contextual text links and paid inclusion), rich media (including video), classified ads, sponsorships, referrals (lead generation) and e-mail (embedded ads only); excludes mobile ad spending; *also called referrals
Source: eMarketer, October 2007

088301   www.eMarketer.com

Figure 19 - US Online Advertising Spending by Format, 2006-2011 (Hallerman, Search Engine Marketing:, 2008)

Basically there are two forms of search engine marketing: the search engine optimization and the search engine advertising. The Search Engine Optimization (SEO) is the process of editing and organizing the content and the structure of a website in order to improve the ranking in organic search results pages (MarketingTerms.com; SearchCIO-Midmarket). These results are ranked by the relevance of certain keywords: the first step of the SEO process is just in selecting a group of relevant keywords to be emphasized in the website. This is accomplished through different techniques, like HTML tags, page layout, site's architecture, links to and from external pages, name of the web pages and of the domain. The importance of the domain is often underestimated: Internet marketing expert Bill Sweetman dedicated a blog[35] to review films' domains, pointing out their effectiveness to attract potential audience and to be listed in search engines.

The Search Engine Advertising is the placement of an advertising in search engine result pages, which is linked to a specific keyword or phrases: the purchase of these keywords grant the website to be listed in the page every time a user search for them. The listing could be on the top of the page, before the organic results, or through banners on the

---

[35] http://www.hollywoozy.com

side of the page. The price of the bidding is usually based on two factors: the pay-per-click, that is the amount of money to pay for each person who clicks on the ad, and the click-through-rate, that is the number of users that actually click on the ad divided by the number of users that see it on the search result page. There are several advantages of SEA that has determined its popularity: the possibility to establish in advance a budget of the advertising campaign and set the bidding as a consequence, being able to customize every aspect of keywords, like interval of hours, days and so on and above all, deliver the advertising message to an highly targeted segment of audience (Thilk, The Week in Movie Search: 8/10/07, 2007; Thilk, Who won the Search Bowl, 2008).

9. Widget Marketing

A *"widget"* can be defined as a small application that displays any kind of content or utility. There are two types of widgets (Pishevar, 2006), the desktop and the web ones. The desktop widgets (also called widgets) are downloaded from the Internet and installed physically on the computer of the user, providing him a service (weather forecast, calculator, etc.) or simply some fun (games, video, audio, etc.).

Web widgets (Lal, 2007) are actually the more common category, and they are a ready-to-use code that can be easily embedded and executed in any HTML page without requiring any additional compiling: they basically allow to grab content from a website and add it to a web page, a blog or a social network profile.

Widget and the so called "widget marketing" has become the last trend of online marketing, and eMarketer estimates (Williamson, Web Widgets and Applications: Destination Unknown, 2008) that in 2008 U.S. companies will spend up to $40 million for creating and distributing web widgets, that are seen as an evolution of the old-fashioned banner ads in the mission of spreading the awareness of the brand and, above all, drive traffic into the brands' websites.

Figure 20 - US Web Widget and Application Advertising Spending, 2007 & 2008 (Williamson, Web Widgets and Applications: Destination Unknown, 2008)

Why the web widgets are becoming so popular? There are several reasons, which concern the characteristics of this tool and the recent trends that involved the Web (Yared, 2008; Ahern, 2008). A widget has an intrinsic viral nature: the simplicity of grabbing a widget, posting it and sharing with friends allows the publisher to benefit from a virtually free distribution, letting the users to become promoters and distributors of the content; users that post a branded widget on their website are actually agreeing to place an unpaid ad for that brand so it has to offer a very attractive content (Thilk, Bringing widgets to your movie marketing efforts, 2007). Besides being interesting, widgets are also interactive, and players usually spend time "playing" with it. The engagement of the customer is what differentiate the banner from the widget: banners are like online billboards seen while users are "driving" through the Internet, widgets are like cool applications on the users' computer board, that are promoting a brand or a product but at the same time they offer something useful (or enjoyable) to users.

From the other side advertising in the Internet through banners has become way more difficult. The share of online advertising on the media spending is yearly increasing from the 6% in the 2006 to an estimated 10% in 2009 (Hallerman, US Online Advertising: Resilient in a Rough Economy, 2008) so are the cost of an impression (that is placing an ad). At the same time, the over-exposure of web users to banners originated a phenomenon called "banner-ad blindness" (Nielsen, 2007) which simply means that surfers ignore everything that looks like a banner. The shift in consumer behaviour from a push-type advertising like banners to a pull-type one like web widgets is the same of what happens in another media that reached an overload exposition of advertising: the TV. An overwhelming offering of TV channels strewn with advertising created a market for digital video recorders like TiVo, that allows the user to select what to watch, filtering all the advertising.

Widgets, besides being the advertising's counterattack to the banner-ad blindness, are also deployed for penetrating the growing market of social networks. According to eMarketer, in 2008 43.5% of adult Internet users are also Social Network Users, while the percentage rockets to 77% for teens (eMarketer, 2008). Brands focus their efforts in creating widgets that offer an extra value to Social Networks' users, persuading them to embody and post the widget on their Profile pages, which in the Web 2.0 is the place where Internet users spend a lot of their time.

Top 10 Web Widget Audiences in the US, Ranked by Unique Viewers, November 2007 (thousands and % of total Internet users)		
	Unique viewers	% of Internet users
1. MySpace	57,747	31.7%
2. Slide	39,213	21.5%
3. Clearspring*	39,159	21.5%
4. RockYou!	32,557	17.9%
5. Photobucket	26,434	14.5%
6. Google	19,436	10.7%
7. BunnyHeroLabs	16,123	8.8%
8. MusicPlaylist.us	15,844	8.7%
9. MyPlaylist	15,586	8.5%
10. BlingyBlob	14,967	8.2%
Total widget audience in the US	**147,904**	**81.1%**

Note: home, work and university locations; widgets are defined as embedded flash (.swf) objects; includes individual widgets, not the platforms that deliver them; excludes desktop widgets; Facebook is excluded from the list due to different measurement methodology; *total includes widget platform and independent objects
Source: comScore Widget Metrix as cited in press release, January 24, 2008

091745   www.eMarketer.com

Figure 21 - Top 10 Web Widget Audiences in the US

A critique to this approach is the article *"Why widgets Don't Work"* (Kunz, 2008) where Ben Kunz warns marketers from investing all their efforts in widget marketing strategies to conquer the Social Networks' audiences. The point is in how users spend their time on the Web: Google users are actually "hunting" for information, so providing it through advertising is highly effective and part of the "core" activity. At the opposite, users are in social networks for having interactions with other people, so even if they use an interesting widget, this will not create awareness for the brand, since it is a diversion, not part of the core activity. The difference is on the mindset: "*A Google user is walking into a store. A Facebook user is walking into a bar*".

Nevertheless, if the brand is able to target his segment of audience with a compelling message\content, appealing and leveraging to the interests and values of the users, the widget marketing can be effective also in social networks environments. For example, for the launch of the vampire horror movie *30 Days of Night*, Sony Pictures partnered with the Facebook application (that is actually a widget that works in the Facebook environment) *Vampires*, an RPG (role-playing game) that had already a customer base of over 3 million of user. Sony re-branded the application with film graphics and launched a sweepstake contest: in over 3 weeks the sweepstakes reached 59,100 entries and the visits were 11,642,051. In order to explain this success, Jeremiah Owyang suggests that Sony identified the segment of audience of its films and targeted the community leveraging on an existing application and a broad fans base ("*Fishing where the fish are*") and also the studio "*compliment the existing user experience*" offering extra value through prizes and improved game experience (Owyang, Case Study: How Sony Leveraged A Popular "Vampire" Facebook Widget To Reach It's Community, 2008).

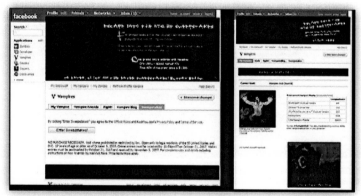

Figure 22 - Vampire Facebook Widget (Owyang, Case Study: How Sony Leveraged A Popular "Vampire" Facebook Widget To Reach It's Community, 2008)

This and other successful executions of widget marketing help to define some useful principles that publisher should follow (Thilk, Bringing widgets to your movie marketing efforts, 2007):

- *Add Value*: in order to get free distribution of the widget, publishers should provide through the widget some kind of value for the user, in order to persuade him to post it in his webpage.
- *Don't push them away*: widget should allow navigating through the content within the window, and avoid redirecting the user to another website. Users will not post a widget the push the traffic away from their website.
- *Stay on target*: before launching a widget, the publisher should carefully identify the segment of audience of the brand\product promoted and create a content that will appeal to that specific target. A content that mismatches with the brand\product values will only confuse the users and then fail.
- *Respect the sidebar*: the size of the widget's window should fit the available space in the user's page. Instead of creating a widget that pops up invading the rest of the page (like some annoying ad banners), it's better to design widgets of different sizes.

Figure 23 - Choice of Size for the 007 Quantum of Solace's Widget (*http://www.007.com/widget/*)

- *Be platform agnostic*: the reason of being of a widget is to be shared and go viral, so publishers should make as easy as possible the sharing, offering different versions for each platform.

III. The assessment of the online Marketing tools

Introduction

The previous chapter presented the online marketing tools from a theoretical perspective, providing definitions and a classification of the tools in different categories. The purpose of this chapter is building a bridge between the theory behind the tools and the empirical analysis, providing a guideline on how each marketing tool will be evaluated according to its features. The evaluation principles are divided into the tools' categories, and involve only a qualitative assessment, since the details of the methodology are presented in the Exhibit 1.

1. Official Website & User Generated Content

For what it concerns the *official website*, the **content** evaluation is based on the presence on the website of all the sections described in the dedicated paragraph, and the deepness of the information and the material provided:

- *Weak*: the website lacks of some sections and\or the information\content provided are inadequate;
- *Fair*: almost all the sections are displayed, with basic information that covers each of them;
- *Good*: all the sections of the website provide to the user a complete and satisfactory set of information about the film.

- *Excellent*: the website offers all the basic sections and also some extra features not common in other website, the information\content is above the average in quantity and quality.

The **look** is valuated according to the visual experience offered and its relevance with the film content:

- *Weak:* the aspect of the website is poor, without any reference to the look of the film;
- *Fair:* the website is simple but tries to connect with the aspect of the film;
- *Good:* animations and graphics from the movie grant to the user a surfing experience through the website that recalls the film content;
- *Excellent:* a heavy use of animations, graphics and video effects provide the user a remarkable experience through the content of the film.

The *User Generated Content* can be used on websites as a stand-alone feature to enrich the surfing experience or inside a contest or a sweepstake. A frequent UGC on film websites are fan art exhibitions, where users are invited to submit a creative effort about the film that will be published on the website (in this section will be analyzed UGC published also in other official film platforms, like social networks' profiles).

The evaluation starts with a description of the type of UGC used (contest\sweepstake, fan art, other) with the following qualitative judgement:

- *Weak*: there is an insufficient engagement of the user and little/no creative expression;
- *Fair:* there is an attempt to engage the user in a creative effort;
- *Good:* there is an actual engagement of the user for creating something related to the film;
- *Excellent:* there is a superb engagement of the user and a strong expression of his creativity.

If available, the number of entries of the contest/sweepstake is a valuable indicator of the success of the tool.

The assessment of the community acknowledgement is accomplished through the description of the tools used (usually *wikis*, forums, webrings) and its evaluation, that is based on a overall judgement of the effectiveness of the tool(s) used in engaging the community, in a range from *weak*, that is the ineffectiveness of the tools, to *excellent*, which is the implementation of a community acknowledgement strategy that involves different tools.

A quantitative indicator of the effectiveness of the official website in representing a portal for movie infoseekers could be the *Technorati URL Search*: given the address of a website (technically defined URL), the search engine will browse in the blogosphere all the blogs that links to it. The number of blogs that refers to the official website indicates how it is strong in providing information and content to the web community, of whom the blogs are the main publishing medium.

2. Social Networking Websites

Movie marketing on social network websites can be analyzed through an assessment of the presence of film-related profiles on the main networks, such as MySpace and Facebook.

For what it concerns MySpace and Facebook, besides the number of friends\fans of the profile page and the number of comments\wall posts, the quality of the content can be classified in:

- *weak:* the profile displays some basic information about the film and little\no multimedia content;
- *fair:* the profile displays a lot of information and some multimedia content like videos and images, all from the official website;
- *good:* the profile has all the material published on the website and in the online marketing campaign, adding to the multimedia content also some extra features like games and downloads;

- *excellent:* besides having all the material published on other platforms, there are some specific content designed for the social network platform, and a customized page with original material.

Only for Facebook, the analysis continues on the presence of Facebook Gifts and of Facebook Applications. These can be evaluated by the number of active monthly users, fans and quality of the content:

- *weak:* the application provides little\no interaction with the film content;
- *fair:* the application provides some basic experience with the film content;
- *good:* the application involve the user in the film experience, allowing him to play with film related content;
- *excellent:* the application offers an experience that fully recalls the plot of the film.

If the film is promoted on other social network websites, this presence is valuated with the same principles above mentioned for Facebook and MySpace pages, plus some quantitative referrals about the engagement of that community, like number of friends or adopters of the film content.

3. Syndicated Content

Blogs can be evaluated by the total number of posts of the blog, the frequency of the updates (daily, weekly, every two weeks, etc.), the time extension of the blog (some blog lasts for just few months, others for years), with how many websites\platforms the posts can be shared (that is important to generate links to the blog), and evaluation of the content posted:

- *Weak:* the blog is uninteresting and provides little\no information to the audience and it is not written by someone directly involved in the production of the film;
- *Fair:* the blog provides some kind of information, and is written by someone involved in the production, like a production assistant or co-producer;

- *Good:* the blog is updated by the filmmaker with first quality news on the production of the film;
- *Excellent:* the blog is updated by the filmmaker using also multimedia content, like video and images from the production

The ideal film blog starts at the very beginning, when the project is approved, is written by one of the filmmakers, frequently updated with multimedia content that can be easily shared on many different platforms.

The podcast is also evaluated by the total number of uploads and their frequency; the content podcasted is:

- *Weak:* few videos that can be easily found elsewhere, like trailers and TV commercials;
- *Fair:* a collection of promoting videos, like trailers and TV commercials, and some extra ones, like interviews or parties
- *Good:* a full series of videos like behind the scenes or interviews with the cast and the talents, plus clips from the film
- *Excellent:* a full collection of all types of video, behind the scenes, interviews, clips, trailers and all kind of video material related to the film.

The research of film podcasts is performed mainly through iTunes, which is one of the main platforms of podcast management.

4. Mobile Marketing

The mobile downloads can be categorized in ringtones, wallpapers and others, reporting also the total number of items available for the download. Another indicator is the presence of a mobile-friendly version of the official website. For what it concerns the mobile games, the evaluation can be:

- *weak:* the game uses very little film content, offering a very basic gameplay;

- *fair:* the gameplay involves some content from the film with a simple gameplay;
- *good:* players can using all film content related and the gameplay offers a good gaming experience;
- *excellent:* besides a total integration with film content, the gameplay strictly recalls the plot and the story of the film.

If the mobile marketing campaign involves other tools, these are evaluated like always according to the relevance with the film and the targeted audience, from *weak* to *excellent.*

5. Advergaming

The web-based games (or online promotional games) are evaluated by the relevance of the gameplay with the film, besides quantifying their number:

- *weak:* the game uses very little film content, offering a very basic gameplay;
- *fair:* the gameplay involves some content from the film with a simple gameplay;
- *good:* players can using all film content related and the gameplay offers a good gaming experience;
- *excellent:* besides a total integration with film content, the gameplay strictly recalls the plot and the story of the film.

Another indicator is the presence of in-game advertising, that is judged by players as a proof of being a cutting-edge brand, and of a spin-off videogame, which promotion amplify the buzz around the release of the film.

For what concerns the Alternative Reality Games is not easy to find evaluation criteria and moreover quantifiable results. An easy-to-find data is the span of time of the game, and a list of the media platforms where the game is developed: these could be the web, mobile, billboards, TV, real time events and others. If available, a great indicator of the success of a promotional ARG is the number of players involved.

6. Cross Brand Promotion

A first indicator of the cross brand marketing of films is the types of marketing tools used by partners, which could be mini-sites, contests, UGC contests and others. Then, a quantitative indicator of the number of partners combined with a qualitative evaluation of the relevance of the partners with the segments of the audience of the film, is a good clue of the type of approach adopted by the film, if a quantity or a quality one; the evaluation is also on the involvement of the partners in the active promotion of the film:

- *Weak:* there is no correlation between the choice of partners and the film's audience, with little promotional efforts of the brands;
- *Fair:* there is some correlation between some partners and segments of audience and some efforts of the brands for promoting the movie;
- *Good:* almost all of the partners have a correlation with a segment of the audience, also investing resources for actively promoting the film;
- *Excellent:* all the partners have been chosen for a direct correlation with a specific segment of audience, with remarkable efforts of each of them to promote the film.

Since the purpose of this analysis is exploring the online marketing strategies in promoting films, brands that offered only an offline support will not be considerate, but only the promotional partners that have implemented any kind of internet marketing tools.

7. Viral Marketing

The viral message can be evaluated by listing the locations of the interactive platform (website, social network, mobile, other) and the number of sharing options, that is extremely important for make it go viral. About the message, this can be judged by his relevance to the film content and the overall quality, which can be defined as a mix of originality and complexity of the message, from *weak* to *excellent:*

- *Weak:* the message is little relevant with the film and is very simple;

- *Fair:* the message is relevant with the film and presents some content related;
- *Good:* the message uses multimedia content to spread the buzz, in a original way;
- *Excellent:* the message uses multimedia content, with original material from the film and also with the direct participation of the user (like UGC).

If the campaign uses other viral marketing tools (like videos, fake blogs, and fake news) this are listed and evaluated with the same scale of the viral message, from *fair* to *excellent.*

The result of the viral marketing (and the overall online campaign) is the creation of the buzz around the movie, which can be roughly measured counting how many blogs talk about the film. Blogs are the main expression of the audience's thoughts and opinions, so the number of blogs could be an indicator of the spreading of the buzz.

The first two blog search engines of the web are *Google Blog Search* and *Technorati Blog Search*: the search will be performed with the exact title of the film plus "film OR movie". For film titles that refer to common words, some specific variation of the search will be applied to reduce the bias, like for example the dates when the blogs were written, including the name of the main actor or director. Including so specific criteria for the search will display fewer results, with the possible bias of excluding some blogs, but in order to perform this analysis is more acceptable under-estimate the blogosphere then over-estimate.

For example, the blog search for the James Bond film *"Casino Royale"* will be performed trying to include words related to the film, in order to exclude results related to other arguments that share a so common title:

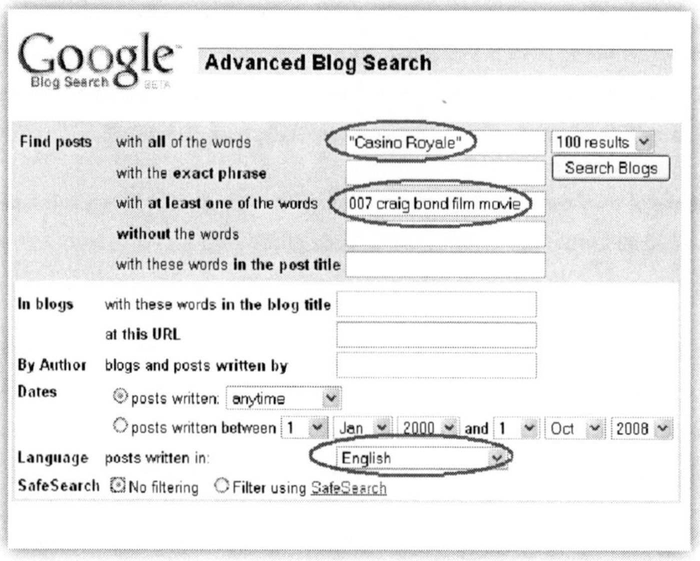

Figure 24 - Example of Google Blog Search

8. Search Engine Marketing

A simple assessment of a deployment of the search engine marketing by Hollywood Studios could be typing on Google the title of the film released, and check the results both in the organic results and in paid advertising. Google is a good benchmark since its market share on US total searches is of 63%, versus a 19.6% of Yahoo!, the main (and only) competitor (Kafka, 2008).

For what it concerns the organic search, like mentioned above, an indicator is the ranking obtained by the film typing its title on Google. The paid one reports simply the presence or not of Google ad banners after typing the title of the film.

9. Widget Marketing

The widget can be evaluated counting in how many platforms can be shared and judging the content offered:

- *Weak:* the widget offers a poor content, redirecting the user to the main website for any other material;
- *Fair:* the widget offers some content within the window, like trailers, pictures and other;
- *Good:* the widget offers a wide array of multimedia content or presenting exclusive content that differs from the one offered in the website;
- *Excellent:* the widget presents a rich offer of content, with a rich navigation through it that represents an alternative to visit the website, creating a complementary experience.

IV. The Empirical Analysis

The study of the online marketing campaigns of films requires fresh data: usually after the release in theatres, the online tools deployed to market the film start fading away, and after few weeks a lot of them, such as promotions, sweepstakes or viral websites, are removed from the Internet.

For this reason the sample of films analyzed has been collected observing the Top 25 films in the U.S. box office from the weekend of the 8 August, 2008 to the weekend of the 10 October, 2008. All the box office data has been collected using the Pro version of *Internet Movie Database*[36], one of the most authoritative resources in the motion picture industry.

For what concerns the research of the different components of each film's marketing campaign, a precious source has been the blog *Movie Marketing Madness*[37], where the author Chris Thilk posts reviews of marketing campaigns of some of the films released in the American theatres. The rest of the information is obtained through an extensive direct research on search engines, like *Google*.

The final online marketing scorecard[38], on which the analysis is based, reports basically two groups of information: the first one are the above described *IMDb* data, such as the box office in the first weekend of release, the cumulative box office at the end of the third weekend and the production budget; this data will be used to build different rankings of

---

[36] http://pro.imdb.com/

[37] http://www.moviemarketingmadness.com/blog/

[38] That can be found on Exhibit 2 in a summarized form.

the film. The second type of data are the evaluation points assigned to each category of tools of the online marketing campaign, that have been obtained evaluating the features of each tool and weighting them according to their importance. The scores of the nine tools are weighted and summed to obtain a final score (in a scale from 0 to 7), that summarize in one unique value the quality of the online marketing campaign.[39]

Observing the final scores, no one of the 66 films analyzed has obtained 5, 6 or 7 points, and only the 3.03 % has gained a score from 4 to 5 points. This is explainable by the complexity and the extension of the tools proposed, and also by the fact that each marketing campaign usually focuses on some tools and ignores others, according to the target of audience. The 22.73% of the films had a score between 3 and 4 points, 25.76% between 2 and 3 points and the most numerous classes of films (39.39%) obtained from 1 to 2 points. Only 6 movies (9.09%) had an insufficient score from 0 to 1 point.

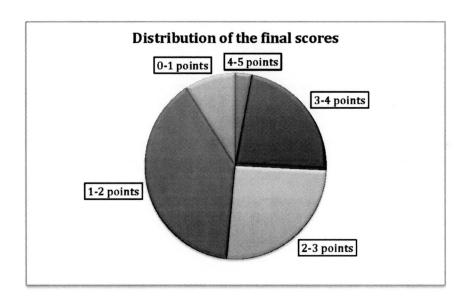

Figure 25 - Distribution of the online marketing scores in the sample

---

[39] The methodology is described in the Exhibit 1

In the following paragraphs the films of the sample will be ranked according to different criteria, such as box office results and production budgets. Each ranking will be followed by the analysis of the distribution of the final scores and the correlation between the ranking criterion and the final scores. The goal is finding some explanations of the different quality among the online marketing campaigns deployed, and the degree of connection between the quality of the campaign and the box office results of the film.

1. Release Weekend's Box Office Ranking

Destiny of films is almost always decided after the release weekend: a positive box office result will grant a longer permanence in the theatres, scattering a virtuous effect: a successful film fosters the positive word of mouth and buzz, that attracts more audience, that convince the theaters to keep the film running, that give the possibility to other people to watch the film and so on. A negative release weekend instead has the completely opposite effects, and it often implies a shorter theatrical life, reducing dramatically the possibility to cover the loss. Statistically speaking, in the sample of 66 films analyzed, the box office in the release weekend accounted in average for the 40.19% of the box office result cumulated after three weeks.

This first classification implies ranking the 66 films of the sample according to their box office results at the end of the weekend of release, from the best performing, that is *The Dark Knight*, to the worst one, the documentary *Man on Wire*. The distribution of the final scores assumes the aspect described in this chart (the extended version could be found in the Exhibit 3):

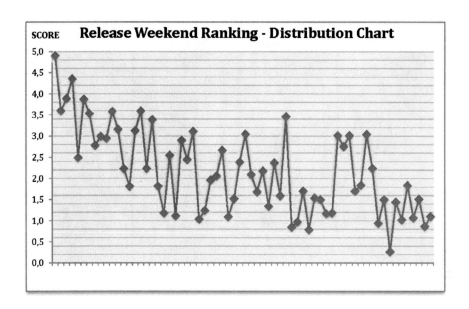

Figure 26 - Distribution chart in the release weekend ranking

In order to get some insights on the performance of these films, it is useful to divide the distribution into four quartiles[40], and pinpoint for each quartile the best performing film and the worst one, with the purpose of identifying in the tools' evaluations the causes of the online marketing campaign final score. While some of the films have evaluations in line with the distribution, others present slightly different scores, which deserve a further deepening.

---

[40] Since the sample is composed by 66 films, each quartile should be of 16.5 films: the decision is to assign 16 films each to the first two quartiles and 17 films each to the last two quartiles.

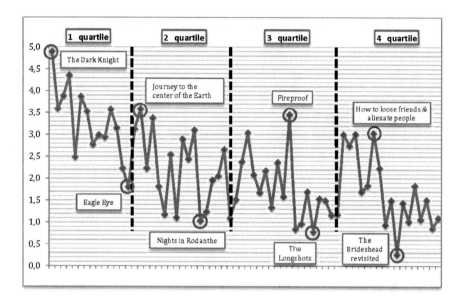

Figure 27 · Quartiles' Chart in the Release Weekend Ranking

In the first quartile, the best performing film is *The Dark Knight,* and the worst *Eagle Eye. The Dark Knight* achieved a box office result in its release weekend of $158,411,483, with an online marketing score of 4.89 points. In order to explain this score, it is useful to compare the scores of the components of *The Dark Knight*'s campaign with the other films in the first quartile[41]: it under performs only in the Syndicated Content (0.00 vs. 0.37 of average) and in the Widget Marketing (3.5 vs. 3.72 of average), while over performing in all the other tools. In particular, in the Mobile Marketing and Viral marketing categories, *The Dark Knight* obtained the best scores of all the 66 films: the credit of this performance goes to a rich offer of content for the mobile platform (such as a wide array of downloads, a mobile game, a mobile version of the official website and an *iPhone* application), and in particular way to the Alternative Reality Game[42] that ran over the 15 months prior to the release and involved millions of players both online and offline. All the viral material created, the buzz generated by the game and the attention received by

---

[41] The average box office result in the first quartile is of $58,522,220

[42] http://whysoserious.com/

media were good explanations to the success of the online marketing campaign and to the achievement of the box office result. For what concerns *Eagle Eye* it gained 1.81 points with a box office result of $29,150,721: its online marketing campaign is particularly strong in the Advergaming category (4.64 points vs. 3.41 of average), thanks to two interactive games ("Eagle Eye Free Fall"[43] and "Eagle Eye Experience"[44] that involve the user in the movie experience: unfortunately, in the scorecard advergaming accounts only for the 9% of the final score, and the film under performs in much more important categories like the Official Website (1.69 points vs. 3.44 of average), Search Engine Marketing (5.00 vs. 6.38 of average) and Widget Marketing (0.00 vs. 3.72).

In the second quartile the best performing film is *Journey at the center of the Earth* and the worst performing is *Nights in Rodanthe*. *Journey at the center of the Earth* earned 3.38 points with a box office of $21,018,141 and its online marketing has its strengths in Widget Marketing (5.5 points vs. 2.56 of average) and in the Syndicated Content. The "Flip Side" movie widget[45] presents an interesting feature with a strong relevance with the film's plot: users can enter their ZIP code and find out what is the exact polar opposite, with also a short description of the place; the Syndicated content involves instead a blog called "The Vernian Logs"[46] particularly rich of entries about scientific-like arguments. The performance of *Nights in Rodanthe* is not particularly inferior to the other low performing film of the quartile, except for a particularly low profile official website (0.55 points vs. 1.89 of average).

In the third quartile there is the interesting case of the film *Fireproof*, that even if ranks in the 41st place as box office result in the release weekend, it has a particularly strong online marketing campaign with a score of 3.45 points (9th in the all sample), that is superior to all the films in the third quartile and also in the second quartile. There are two particular strengths of this online marketing campaign: the first one is the official website (3.45 points vs. 1.84 of average) that corresponds exactly to the definition of the official website as a *portal* of information for infoseekers: in *fireproofthemovie.com* users

---

[43] http://eagleeyefreefall.com/

[44] http://experience.eagleeyemovie.com/

[45] http://www.journey3dmovie.com/widget/widget.html

[46] http://www.progressivevolcanology.com/

finds all type of resources connected with the film, and it works as a start point for all the other marketing efforts. Another unique feature of the website is the so called "Take Action" section[47] of the website, where there is a truly empowerment of the audience to promote and market the film themselves, online through banners, widgets and email signatures, offline through initiatives to bring the film in local theatres of the audience. The second strength is the official movie blog (Syndicated Content 4.78 vs. 0.61 points of average), that started first as a production blog[48] and then as a movie-related news blog[49], offering an impressive number of 135[50] posts over a period of 11 months, and is kept posted even months after the release in theatres. Indeed, the 41st place in the release weekend box office ranking is just a first look to the overall results of the film, which will be further explored in the next rankings. The worst performing film of the third quartile is instead *The Longshots* with 0.78 points, which besides having an (insufficient) official website and a fair ranking in the organic search engine results, has no other online marketing efforts.

The fourth quartile presents as best performing film *How to loose friends & alienate people*, that despite presenting a good online marketing campaign (with 3.04 points, 15th place in the ranking by online marketing scores) resulted in a disappointing box office during the release weekend: in the same situation there are other two films, *City of Ember* (3.01 points and 16th place) and *College* (3.01 points and 17th place). All these three films presented at the same time above the average online marketing campaign scores and weak box office results, a fact that confirm the complexity of the film product and the substantial unpredictability of the results: in this particular case the explanation could be probably found in factors beyond the online marketing campaign, that are not subject of these analysis. The worst performing film is *The Brideshead revisited*, that owns its score (0.26 points) to the actual absence (among the first 100 websites) in the search engine results of the official website, the only (weak) effort of online marketing.

---

[47] http://www.fireproofthemovie.com/takeaction/

[48] http://fireproofproduction.blogspot.com/

[49] http://fireproofthemovie.blogspot.com/

[50] 34 posts in the 2007 and 101 posts in the 2008, last post updated on the 24th October 2008.

Analyzing the two series of variables in the sample from a statistic perspective, at a first sight there seems to be a connection between the box office performance in the release weekend of the films and the score of their online marketing campaigns. In order to explore this hypothesis, the following chart shows the distribution of the scores according to the box office results, drawing a line of tendency (also called regression line) of the succession of points:

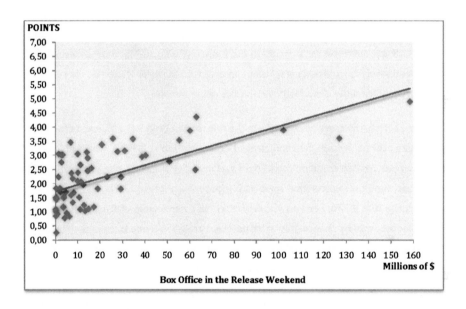

Figure 28 - Correlation Chart in the Release Weekend Ranking

The relation between two variables can be measured by the correlation, which is a single number that describes the degree of relationship between two or more variables. A correlation coefficient can range from a value of -1.00 (that is a perfect negative correlation) to a value of 1.00 (that is a perfect positive correlation); a value of 0 is the absence of correlation. In this particular scenario, the correlation between the release weekend box office result (from the worst to the best) and the online marketing scores (from the worst to the best) is of 0.6689[51]. Before discussing this value, it is necessary to evaluate it, analyzing the two properties of a correlation, that are the *magnitude* (or *strength*) of the correlation and its *significance*.

The *magnitude* is measured by the coefficient of determination, that is the square of the correlation value, and it can range from 0 to 1.00. It estimates the amount of common variation between the two variables: a magnitude coefficient of 1.00 means that there will be a proportional change in the 2nd variable for every change in the first one. The *significance* level instead is the primary indicator about the reliability of the correlation, and it mainly depends by the size of the sample. It basically finds out which is the probability that the observed relationship in the sample is occurred by pure chance. There are several level of significant correlations according to the level of interval chosen (that is the probability above described) and the size of the sample.

Like said before, the correlation between the release weekend box office and the online marketing score is 0.6689. Its coefficient of determination is 0.4475, which means the two variables have in common the 45% of variance. For a sample size of 66 items, the minimum significant correlation level with a probability of 0.005[52] is 0.3112[53], which would mean that if between two variables there is a correlation of 0.3112 there is the 0.5% that occurred by chance. Nevertheless, the correlation found is more than the double of the minimum level significance, which means that is extremely significant (the estimation of the probability is less than 0.0001[54]).

A second level of analysis that gives precious insights on a correlation is the determination of the outliers. Outliers are atypical observations that may have a strong influence on the inclination of the regression line and therefore on the value of correlation itself, and for these reasons their presence reserves further explanations and considerations.

---

[51] This and the following results are obtained through Excel sheets, with the support of the software SPSS 16.0 and some online tools, like http://www.graphpad.com and http://www.quantitativeskills.com/sisa.

[52] The minimum standard of probability for considering a correlation statistically significant is 0.05.

[53] Level of significance for one-tailed test, since it was expected a positive relation between box office results and final scores.

[54] This P is obtained as consequence of a t value of 7.1987 and a degrees of freedom of 64, and is a two-tailed P value (due to restrictions of the calculator)

One of the most common quantitative method for detecting the outliers is the Grubb's test, also called the E.S.D. method (Extreme Studentized Deviate): it consists in finding a value called Z[55] for each of the data of the distribution and comparing it with a critical Z value, that can be found according to the population of the sample and the P value (that is the probability described above for the significance level).

The sample of films analyzed presents a critical Z value of 3.5984, calculated with significance level of 0.01[56] (P value): of all the 66 values, no one has a Z value greater than the critical Z value, so it is possible to conclude that there are no significant outliers.

It is therefore possible to confirm that there is a significant correlation between the two variables observed, that means that the quality of the online marketing campaign of a film can positively affect the box office results during the release weekend.

2. Production Budget Ranking

In the last three years, the average total cost per film in the U.S. market is slightly increased (MPAA, 2008), moving from an average of $99.7 million in the 2005 to the $106.6 million in the 2007[57]. Of these total expenditures, about one third is of marketing costs, a proportion that has demonstrated to remain constant in the recent years: it is therefore possible to state a rule of thumb that given a production budget for a film, studio is probably willing to dispose a marketing budget that amounts to half of the production budget:

---

[55] The Z ratio is calculated as the difference between the value and the mean of the distribution divided by the standard deviation of the distribution.

[56] This P value is double-sided, due to restrictions of the calculator used.

[57] These data represents the Average U.S. Theatrical cost per MPAA members.

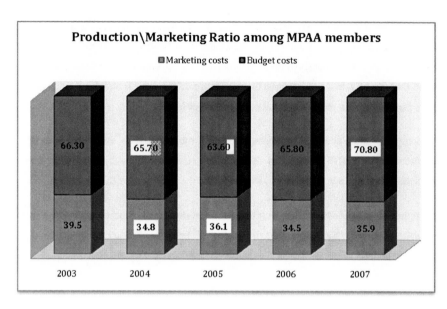

Figure 29 - Production\Marketing Ratio among MPAA members

For what concerns the online marketing analysis while the marketing incidence on the overall costs is stable, the incidence of Internet Advertising on the total advertising expenditures of the MPAA Members is continuing to grow, moving from the 2.4% in the 2004 to the 4.2% in 2007. An even more strong growth is reported for the MPAA Member Subsidiaries/Affiliates, from a 2.4% in the 2004 to the 5.3% of 2007:

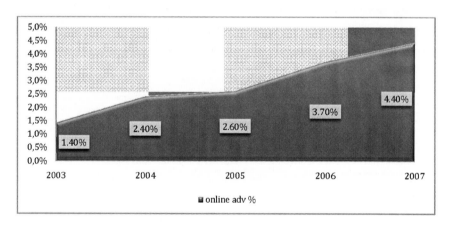

Figure 30 - Positive increase of online advertising in MPAA members

There is indeed a steady ratio between the production and the marketing budget, while a growing percentage of the marketing budget is spent for online marketing. In the sample of 66 films analyzed, it has been possible to collect information only about the production budget, but due to the relationship above described, the assumption is that an amount correspondent to a percentage of the production budget is spent for online marketing. For these reasons, the ranking here proposed will order the films from the biggest production budget to the smallest one, with the expectation that a bigger production budget correspond to a bigger online marketing budget, with the consequence of more resources available for deploying a better online marketing campaign.

Unfortunately, in the sample analyzed it was not possible to collect the production budget for 10 of the 66 films analyzed. The films with the biggest production budget are *The Dark Knight* and *Indiana Jones and the Kingdom of the crystal skull*, both quoted at $185,000,000, the smallest production budget is $50,000 for *Fireproof*. The distribution of the films' final scores according to the size of the budget, from the biggest to the smallest is the following:

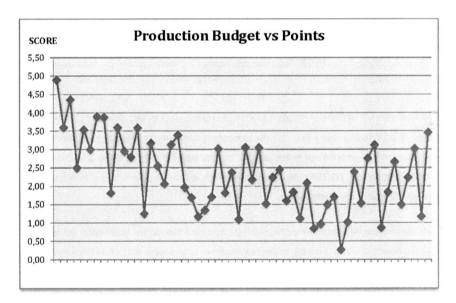

Figure 31 - - Distribution Chart in the Production Budget Ranking

At a first sight, this distribution seems to have a tendency slightly different from the previous one: the online marketing scores seem to decrease according to the production budget, but at the end of the distribution this tendency gives the impression to reverse. In order to better comprehend this effect, it is possible to draw a polynomial type of tendency line, with a division of the chart in four quartiles (composed by 14 films each):

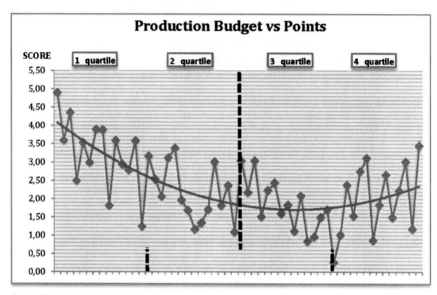

Figure 32 - Quartiles' Chart in the Production Budget Ranking

The first quartile of films presents an average score of 3.25 points, the second one an average of 2.17 points, the third one an average of 1,86 points while the last one, as expected, presents an average score of 1.98 points, superior to the third quartile. Before introducing further considerations on these data, it is advisable to analyze the correlation coefficient of the distribution.

The correlation between the production budget and the online marketing scores is of 0.6199, which is a little inferior to the correlation of the scores with the release weekend box office (0.6689). These two variables have in common the 38.43% of the variance, as indicator of the magnitude of the correlation. The minimum level of significance for a sample size (N) of 56 elements with a probability of p=0.001 is 0.3960[58], so the correlation can be considered as extremely statistically significant. Since the score points are the same that the previous analysis, there is no purpose in performing an outliers detections.[59]

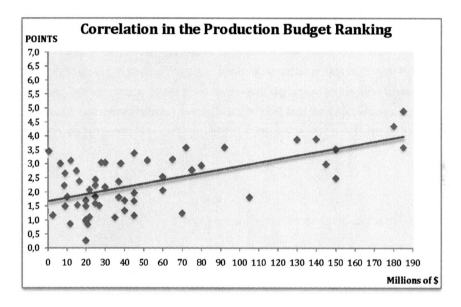

Figure 33 - Correlation Chart in the Production Budget Ranking

Combining the correlation analysis with the considerations about a different behavior of the last quartile of the sample, it is helpful to calculate the correlation excluding the last quartile, since the evidence is of a tendency opposite to the rest of the sample. The correlation coefficient of the first three quartiles (N=42) is of 0.7132, that is superior to the correlation of the whole sample. This correlation is significant[60] and the two variables have the 50.86% of variance in common: the assumption of a different behavior of the films in the last quartile could be considered as true.

---

[58] This level significance refers to a two-tailed test. The level of significance for a one-tailed test, with a p=0.005 and a sample n=56 is 0.3366

[59] The outliers detection is based on the mean and on the standard deviations of the items of the series, all indicators that are not affected by the position in the distribution; the outliers will not be presented again in the other rankings

[60] With a N=42 and a p=0.001 in a two tailed test the minimum level of significance is of 0.4896.

These results imply that in the sample of films analyzed the movies with the lowest budget have deployed average better online marketing campaigns than the ones with an immediately higher production budget. A plausible explanation could be that low budget films are often produced by small independent studios which can not afford television commercials or benefit of important brands' sponsorships. Internet at the opposite has no entry barriers and basically everyone can access to this medium: artsy studios can use their creativity to deploy online marketing campaigns that efficiently target the audience of their films with valuable promotional messages, without disposing of substantial financial resources. The example that explain this strategy is again the film *Fireproof,* that with a production budget of $50,000 has deployed a marketing strategy that scored 3.45 points, based on a strong website, a rich blog and the involvement of the community.

3. Cumulative Box Office at the end of the third weekend

The release weekend has without any doubt a strong influence on the film's overall box office result. Nevertheless, the online marketing campaign has an impact on the moviegoing decision that goes beyond the first weekend, and it affects the whole running of the movie in theatres. For these reasons, the expectation is to have a stronger correlation between the quality of the online marketing campaign and the box office result at the end of three weeks[61] than just at the end of the release weekend. The ranking displays in the first place again *The Dark Knight* with $393,751,065 and in the last one *Beer for my horses* with $411,212. In order to detect the presence of substantial changes in the distribution, the chart will be divided as usually in four quartiles, commenting the noticeable differences with the release weekend's ranking.

---

[61] The choice of three weeks is due to the recent release of some films at the time of this analysis, that does not allow collecting data on a wider period of time.

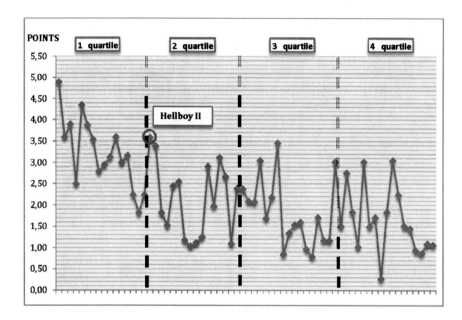

POINTS

| 1 quartile | 2 quartile | 3 quartile | 4 quartile |

Hellboy II

Figure 34 - Distribution Chart divided in quartiles in the 3Weeks Cumulative Box Office

The situation in the first quartile is not changed, *The Dark Knight* has still the top score, and so *Eagle Eye* the bottom one. In the second quartile instead, while *Nights in Rodanthe* keeps the last position, the best performing is not anymore *Journey at the Center of the Earth* (that moves to the 2nd place) but *Hellboy II: The Golden Army*. *Hellboy II* ranked at the 11th position in the release weekend ranking placing itself in the first quartile, but its three weeks performance placed it to the 17th position in the current ranking; its online marketing strategy scores 3.58 points, ranking 7th in the all sample, and achieves the hard goal to market a comics' hero almost unknown to the audience[62]. The strength of its online marketing campaign is the official website that with 5.32 points is the second best of the sample (after the 5.52 points of *The Dark Knight*): the content offered is extremely rich, with also a section of the website dedicated to the fan art (UGC content); the best valuable feature however concerns the community engagement, with the creation of a *wiki*[63] that introduce the audience to the world surrounding the character and

---

[62] In the sample of films analyzed there are 4 movies that are adaptations of comics book: in term of awareness, while *Batman* could be considered as a "first class" superhero, *Iron Man* and *Hulk* does not benefit of the same worldwide recognizability and even less could be said for *Hellboy*.

[63] http://wiki.universalpictures.com/hellboy/index.php/Main_Page

an official *webring*, with downloadable film banners to display on personal pages. The qualitative evaluation of this website (without the quantitative weight) is actually of 6.7 points[64], ranking as the best movie website of the whole sample. The situation in the third and fourth quartile is the same that the release weekend ranking and there are no particular considerations to do.

The statistical analysis between the cumulative box office results at the end of three weeks and the online marketing campaign scores reveals a correlation coefficient of 0.6748, that is the stronger correlation of the three rankings analyzed at this point (0.6689 in the release weekend ranking and 0.6199 in the budget one). The magnitude of this correlation is of 45.54% and it is extremely statically significant.[65]

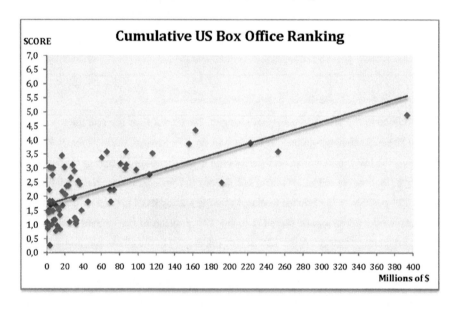

Figure 35 - Correlation Chart in the 3weeks Cumulative Box Office Ranking

---

[64] *Hellboy II*'s website score 6.7 points but the number of URLs linked to it is of 1.717 while *The Dark Knight*'s one, even if the qualitative score is of only 4.95 points, generates a number of links of 5,580, that explains the difference between the final scores of the two films.

[65] The size sample is the same of the release weekend ranking, so all the previous assumptions about the significance can be applied also to this ranking.

This correlation index demonstrates that the online marketing campaigns have an influence that goes beyond the release weekend, affecting the box office result of the film during all his theatrical run. This improvement can be explain by the wide range of factors that could affect the box office performance during the release weekend that may not come up again in the following ones: a typical example of "disturbing factor" is the release of another film that targets the same audience in the same weekend or in the one before, creating a shared audience between the two films, an effect that is not correlated to the quality of the online marketing campaign.

An example of this competition and the box office consequence could be the case of the action comedies *Pineapple Express* and *Tropic Thunder*: according to the ratings of the users of *Internet Movie Database PRO*, these two films have received the same rating (7.7), they are most popular in the same segment of audience (females under 18 years old) with a similar rating (8.8 for *Pineapple Express* and 8.4 for *Tropic Thunder*) and least popular in the same segment (males aged more than 45 years old):

Pineapple Express[66]

Ratings	
• MOVIEmeter:	6
• Average IMDb rating:	7.7 (26,558 votes)
• Most popular:	8.8 - Females under 18 (366 votes)
• Least popular:	6.2 - Males Aged 45+ (517 votes)

Tropic Thunder[67]

Ratings	
• MOVIEmeter:	25
• Average IMDb rating:	7.7 (39,179 votes)
• Most popular:	8.4 - Females under 18 (452 votes)
• Least popular:	7.0 - Males Aged 45+ (1,052 votes)

Figure 36 - Pineapple Express & Tropic Thunder IMDb users' ratings

---

[66] http://pro.imdb.com/title/tt0910936/opinions

[67] http://pro.imdb.com/title/tt0942385/opinions

After these audience's demographics is possible to assume that the films share the same target of audience, like the hypothesis above described. The release weekend of *Pineapple Express* was August 8, 2008 (earning $23,245,025) exactly one week before *Tropic Thunder*, which was released on the weekend of August 15, 2008 when it earned $25,812,796. Despite a superior online marketing campaign, *Tropic Thunder* (3.59 points) in its release weekend performed almost the same of *Pineapple Express* (2.23 points).

After three weeks of theatrical running, the cumulative box office of the two comedies revealed a difference of over $13 million in favor of *Tropic Thunder*, which in the end has demonstrated to the more successful of the two movies. The explanation could be that the effect of the superior marketing strategy could not affect the box office result in the release weekend due to the sharing of the same segment of audience with *Pineapple Express*, released just the weekend before. Nevertheless, the quality of the *Tropic Thunder's* campaign has contributed to the box office results in the long run, resulting in a final cumulative gross superior to the *Pineapple Express'* one.

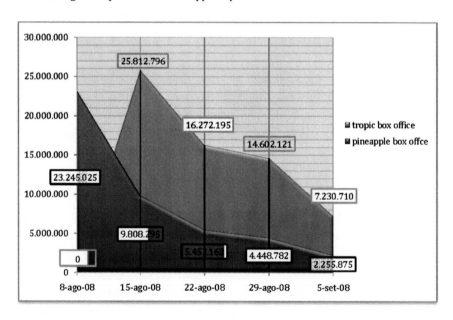

Figure 37 - Pineapple Express & Tropic Thunder Box Office Chart

It is important to point out that the *Tropic Thunder* case is based on assumptions, and there are several factors that could vary the financial results of a movie. However, the correlation analysis has demonstrated that the online marketing campaign has more effect on the cumulative box office than on the first weekend's one, and it is a fact that the audience targeting is affects the decisions of Hollywood studios about the release schedule of films, pursuing the implicit goal to avoid a direct competition between similar movies. For these reasons, the assumptions about the dynamics between *Tropic Thunder* and *Pineapple Express* could be considered probable and worth of attention.

4. Box Office versus Production Budget

Establishing if a film has been successful is a matter of controversy in the film industry: if outstanding successes and crushing failures can be easily picked out, there is a middle zone of box office results that are subjects to interpretation, making difficult to define the benchmark of a financial success.

The solution may come from the production budget, which represents the basic investment made on the film: a first assumption could be that a film is considered successful if it covers the production budget. In the sample of 66 films analyzed, it was possible to collect the production budgets of only 56 of them: of these, 20 had a cumulative box office at the end of the third weekend[68] that covered the production budget, a group that represents the 35.71% of the population. But as mentioned before, the production budget is just a component of the final cost of releasing a film, which comprehends also the marketing expenses. It is possible to assume that the average marketing cost amounts to one third of the production budget[69]: adding this further criterion to the sample, the number of films that cover that total budget (production and marketing) decreases to 15, that is the 26.79% of the sample.

---

[68] It is clear that these films will continue to produce revenues beyond the third weekend, which is only the temporal interval available at the time of this analysis.

[69] Like described in the paragraph " *2.Production budget ranking*"

Nevertheless, stating that only 15 films of the sample are financially successful would be an inaccuracy for two different reasons: the first one is that the revenues taken into consideration refer only to the U.S. theatrical market. A great number of American films are then released in foreign countries and the ones that had a weak opening in the local market could become a success elsewhere, where the tastes of the audience are different or there isn't the strong competition suffered in the U.S. market. The weight of foreign revenues on the total is very different from film to film, according to the genre, the appeal of the cast or the director and many other factors, and it could range from 30% to over 70% of the lifetime gross. For example, the action flick *The Mummy: Tomb of the Dragon Emperor* earned in the U.S. box office a total of $102,176,165[70] against a production budget of $145,000,000: this movie is so excluded from the above described selection of successful films. Nevertheless, *The Mummy*'s third sequel earned another $286,700,000 in foreign markets, representing over the 73% of total revenues.

The second reason is that the theatrical exhibition is just the first of a series of revenues stream, that are the Video/DVD rentals, the Video/DVD retail, the Pay Per View television, the Subscription television and the Free television, all defined as secondary markets. The film continues to generate money over a long time after the theatrical release, with many possibilities for the studios to get back the initial investment, even after a disappointing result in the box office.

The object of this analysis is anyway the online marketing campaign of the films, and since the market of reference is the United States and the marketing tools assessed have as first target the U.S. audience, it is fair to take into consideration only the theatrical results within the U.S., excluding the foreign markets and the other streams of revenues.

Since the online marketing scores demonstrated to be strongly correlated with the release weekend box office, with the production budget and above all with the cumulative box office, a further analysis is the correlation between those scores and the ratio of the box office weighted for the production budget. The success of a film needs to be related to its investment, so the best performing movies are those that give the highest return

---

[70] Data from http://pro.imdb.com, updated at 19 September, 2008.

on investment, and they may be correlated too with the quality of their online marketing campaigns.

Unfortunately, the statistical analysis disclaims this hypothesis: the correlation between the online marketing scores and the release weekend box office weighted for the production budget is of 0.2109 while the correlation between the scores and the ratio between cumulative box office and budget is of 0.2020: both are not statistically significant.[71] So while these ratios could be employed as useful indicators of the theatrical success of the films, like described above, they have no relationships with the online marketing campaigns.

5. Online Marketing & Genre of Films

The previous analysis looked at the online marketing campaign of films as one of the possible explanations of their box office result or at the relationship between its quality and the production budget invested in the film. A further study that can be implemented, this time merely quantitative, involves the genre of the film: the purpose is to explore the possibility that certain genres of movies deploy more frequently some online marketing tools than others.

Define the genre of a film can be extremely difficult, and usually the same movie could belong to more than one categories: *Internet Movie Database*, for example, in its classification uses multiple genres to define a film, up to four, five or even six different categories. Despite a less precise categorization, *Variety* proposes instead a unique genre for each film and it demonstrates to be more suitable for the analysis to be performed. In the sample of 66 films, 16 belong to the *Action* genre, 2 to the *Adventure* genre, 4 to the *Animation* genre, 18 to the *Comedy* genre, 1 to the *Crime* genre, 2 to the *Documentary* genre, 19 to the *Drama* genre, 2 to the *Horror* genre, 1 to *Mystery* and 1 to *Western*. Due

---

[71] The minimum significance level for a population of N=56, with a probability of p=0.05, in a two-tailed test is of r=0.2632.

to a lack of representation for the category, the genres with just one film (*Crime, Mystery* and *Western*) will be not analyzed.

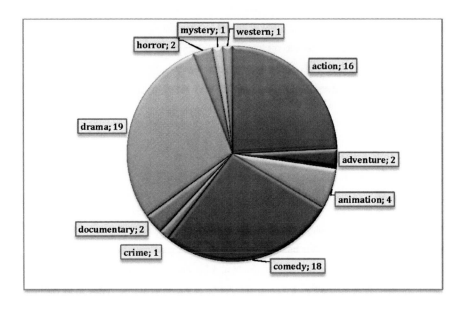

Figure 38 - Distribution of genres in the sample

Action movies are the third most popular genre of films in the sample and they have a superior online marketing campaign score in comparison to the average of the sample (3.01 points vs. 2.18 points). The category of tools deployed can be analyzed comparing their frequency in the genre with the frequency in the sample and comparing the average score in the genre versus the average score in the sample. Combining these two criteria, the online marketing campaigns of action films deploy more frequently and with better results Advergaming[72] and Widget marketing[73]. The use of Advergaming as a ma-

---

[72] Advergaming is used with a frequency superior to the average of the sample of 31.44% and an average score superior of 1.44 points.

[73] Widget marketing is used with a frequency superior to the sample of 28.03% and an average score superior of 1.31 points.

jor online marketing tool of action movies makes perfect sense for two level of compatibility between tool and genre: the first one involves the content of action movies, which can be easily and well represented in video games. The second one is the sharing of the same segment of audience: action films are usually popular among young males that are exactly the segment of the most frequent gamers: according to the ESA (ESA, 2008), 60% of the gamers are male and 25% of them are aged below 18 years. For these reasons, advergaming seems to be the perfect choice to target the audience of action films with a tool that is popular, understood and appreciated by them. The advergaming dynamics explain also the more frequent use of mobile marketing among action movies, superior of 37.12% to the average: part of the mobile marketing involves exactly mobile games, which for a matter of content, are more compatibles with the *action* genre than others.

The *adventure* genre contains only 2 films, making any assumptions devoid of empirical confirmations. Nevertheless, it is noticeable an overall better quality in the advergaming category (1.23 points more than the average), due to the same compatibility of contents and audience described for the action films, and a lack of any cross brand marketing. This could be explained by the characteristics of the genre itself, which often involves fantasy and unrealistic themes that are not appealing to brands for possible partnerships.

The *animation* movies in the sample are 4, and they present a better online marketing score than the average. The peculiarity of this group is that they present a particularly good score in the cross brand marketing category, also by the movies with a weak final score (like the 2.17 points of *Igor* and the 2.37 points of *Space Chimps*): the average score is of 5.10 points versus the average of the sample of 1.79 points. Even if animation movies attracts moviegoers of all ages, they are especially addressed to the youngest segment of audience, that has also a very strong influence on families' consuming decisions: promotional partnerships with these films are extremely attractive to a wide variety of consumer products, that are keen to associate their brands to the favorite movie of kids and teens. The popularity among these audiences may be an explanation of the deployment among animation movies of cause related marketing (classified here as a tool of cross brand marketing): 2 of the 4 movies in the group have associated their brand with a social cause. In particular, *Igor* partnered with *Against Malaria Founda-*

tion[74]: the Igor protagonist of the film lives in the fictional land of Malaria and fights against the evil within his world, trying to change the rules. Using the tagline "*IGOR lives in the land of Malaria but doesn't want anyone else to*", the film worked with the AMF to raise money to buy anti-mosquito nets for African children. The second movie is *Space Chimps*, that partnered with *Animal Planet's Escape to Chimp Eden*[75] to protect the endangered specie of chimpanzees, which are also the protagonist of the film.

Comedy is the second most popular genre and the performance of the online marketing campaigns of the films in this group is slightly inferior to the average of the sample. The frequencies of use of the tools follow very closely the averages of the sample, there is just a slightly less use of Mobile marketing (-10.10%), probably due to the lack of mobile games, and a little more frequency in the Viral marketing (+14.14%), which explanation could be the use of viral messages: comedies are suitable for "funny" messages that involves the content of the movie and are more likely to be sent and spread among friends. For what concerns the quality of the tools they are aligned too with the averages of the sample, with worse results in the Official Website (-0.48 points) and in the Advergaming (-0.47 points). An explanation could be in the common practice of "filling" the website with irrelevant content such as web-based games that, besides having no relevance with the film, cannot fill the lack in the website of primary content, such as cast biographies, well-written plots, exhaustive downloads and so on, causing a weak score in the advergaming category (which is evaluated primarily by the relevance of the games offered with the film content) and in the official website, that should work as an information portal.

The sample collected contains only two *documentaries*, not enough to make any conclusion. Nevertheless, it is possible to observe that both of them have a very weak online marketing campaign, which consists on a basic official website and a minimal presence on social networks: anyway this may be due to the low budget of the two films, and not necessary to a trend of the category.

---

[74] http://www.malaria.com/igor/

[75] http://www.animalplanet.com/spacechimps

Drama is the most popular genre of the sample, with 19 films belonging to this group, that have a mean online marketing score inferior of 0.65 points to the average of the sample. This weakness could be explained by the characteristics of the genre itself, which often involves mature or complex topics that could not be easily used in the marketing material; moreover the segments of moviegoers that represent the typical audience of this genre are older than all the other genres. These tendencies found a confirmation in the empirical results: "non standard" marketing tools like the Mobile marketing, the Viral marketing, Advergaming and Widgets are all less used and are also deployed with an inferior quality and effectiveness, probably due to the consciousness of the marketers about their inefficacy in targeting the audience of *drama* movies. Nevertheless, this cannot be a justification for the weak efforts dedicated in building a good official website and in designing an online marketing strategy: the evidence is again the film *Fireproof*, a drama about a Christian couple with troubles with their marriage, that created a heavy online marketing strategy targeted to married couples and to the Christian community. Movie marketers analyzed the contents of the film (religion and marriage) and then designed online marketing tools that were able to exploit this topics and target the selected segments of audience: an extremely rich and frequent updated blog that had run for almost a year, an official website designed as a portal to the film contents and a community website[76] to expand the contents proposed by the film. All these tools present a great alignment between film-audience-marketing, that is the goal that not only the *drama* but all kind of films should pursue.

The *horror* categories contains only two films, that despite having an average online marketing score aligned with the sample (2.10 points versus 2.18 points), they presents scores and characteristics pretty different: *Mirrors* achieves 1.09 points versus the 3.11 points of *Quarantine*. The audience of *horrors* is for the most part young people and teens, a demographic tendency even stronger than in the *action* genre, so the expectation is to have online marketing campaigns that deploys tools able to deliver the promotional message in these age brackets, like social networks and videogames. Both the movie have an average quality of official website, but *Quarantine* deploys a very strong marketing presence on social networking websites (3.33 points), like it should be for

---

[76] http://www.fireproofmymarriage.com

films targeted to the young audience, and it is one of the two movies[77] of the all sample to be present on four different websites: besides the usual *Facebook* and *MySpace* profiles, *Quarantine* has pages also on *Bebo.com* and *Twitter.com*. According to the expectations, the advergaming category in this movie is particularly developed (4.40 points), with an advanced web-based videogame that greatly fits with the contents of the film, and there is also a viral marketing campaign based on a series of videos posted on a dedicated *YouTube* channel. Even if these assumptions are supported by the scores of only one of the two *horror* films in the sample, it is likely that the online marketing campaign of this genre has its strengths in social networks, advergaming and viral marketing, that appear to be the tools more suitable to target these segments of audience.

---

[77] The other one is *Igor*.

V. Conclusion

This study started by exploring the nature of the film product and establishing the strong need of information that the audience requires for performing the decision of purchase. This need can be satisfied with the help of marketing, which provides information to the moviegoers; among the media that marketing could exploit, the Internet has been chosen as one of the most interesting to observe and also as particularly capable of influencing the decisions of the audience.

This influence of the online marketing campaign on the moviegoing decision has been first explored comparing the quality of the campaigns in the sample (summarized in a score obtained through a scorecard) with the box office in the weekend of release. The release weekend represents the first recognizable result of all the marketing efforts , which are aimed to increase the awareness about the upcoming release among the audience, trying to convince them to go in theatres and watch the film. The correlation statistics has confirmed that there is a highly significant relationship between the online marketing score and the box office result: films that have deployed a good online marketing campaign have good probability to collect a positive box office in the release weekend.

The strength of this first analysis is that the release weekend box office is positively influenced more by the marketing campaign than by other factors: audience knows about the release of the film thanks to marketing or personal research, and selects the film as a consequence. There are not the influencing factors that follow up the release weekend such as the critics' reviews, the peers' word-of-mouth and the same box office result[78], increasing the probability that marketing is one of the most important influencing factors preceding the release. On the other hand considering only the release weekend exposes the results to factors that go beyond the online marketing campaign, and one of

---

[78] A great box office result during the first weekend is often judged by the audience as an indicator of the quality of the film, with a great influence: often astonishing result in the release weekend are then incorporated and used in the marketing campaign, with slogan like "First movie in America" or "Best Comedy of the year".

the most relevant is the competition faced by the release film with movies targeted to the same segment of audience. This phenomenon of shared audience has been explored describing the case of *Tropic Thunder* vs. *Pineapple Express*, both action comedies meant for a teenager audience.

In order to overcome this limit the second analysis expanded the time extension of the box office results, comparing the online marketing score with the cumulative box office at the end of the third weekend of running. This longer period contributed to improve and strengthen the correlation between the two series of variables, representing the best index found in the study: this can be considered as a further evidence of the influence of the online marketing campaign on the moviegoing decisions and on the consequently box office performance. The cumulative box office after three weeks represents with a good accuracy the final domestic box office of the film[79], limiting the distortion caused by competing movies; at the same time after the release weekend the online marketing becomes one of the many factors described above that influences the moviegoing decision.

The previous analysis has considered the box office results, which are consequences of the online marketing campaign. In order to acquire a better comprehension of the phenomenon is useful to enquire the possible causes and determinants of the online marketing campaign, such as the budget of films and the genre.

For what concerns the budget, statistics from the Motion Picture Association of America made possible to establish a relationship between the production budget (that is usually the only available data) and the marketing budget of film, finding also clues about an increased percentage of this marketing budget dedicated to online efforts. This means that bigger production budgets should equal to more resources for the online marketing campaign, with a better result in term of quality; these assumptions have been confirmed by the strong correlation between production budget and the online marketing score. Big budget films seem to have better online marketing campaigns, even if the analysis detected an irregularity: small budget films (belonging to the last quartile of the distribution) presents average scores superior to the small-medium budget films. This

---

[79] In most of the cases the weeks after the third weekend of theatrical run represent a minimal contribution on the overall financial result.

could be explained by small independent studios that thanks to a mix of creativity and cost-efficiency achieve to deploy effective online marketing tools without disposing of Hollywood-sized budget. In conclusion films with substantial budgets are willing to be promoted with good online marketing campaigns, but is not necessarily true the opposite: Internet does not require the considerable financial resources of the other traditional media, making the online marketing tools available even for small production company.

The genre analysis instead classified the film in the samples per genre, in order to observe if the genre has an influence on type and quality of the online marketing tools used. In particular, each genre involves specific kind of contents, having a primary segment of audience that could be an explanation to the distribution of the online marketing scores. The most popular genre is drama, followed by comedy and action, which instead had an average score superior to the sample: action contents can be easily exploited in the marketing campaign, which is aimed to a segment of audience (young people) that seems to be more susceptible to online efforts, such as Advergaming. Other peculiarities are in the animation genre, where the very young audience (kids and children) grants to film promotional deals with national wide brands for cross brand partnerships, especially in consumer products and fast food chain restaurants (the master example are the famous toys in the McDonald's *Happy Meal*); besides commercial companies, animation films often partner with non profit associations, more or less pertinent with the film content, with cause-related marketing initiatives.[80] Horror films instead are probably one of the most favorite genres by teenagers and deploy a strong presence[81] on social networking websites, where the targeted audience spends most of their time. The major limit of the categorization in genres is due to the very complexity of films: it is unusual that a film belong exactly to one category, and more often it can be classified under more genres. Nevertheless, genre helps a lot the marketing of films to create in the audience a clear and distinctive perception of the movie: more it can be

---

[80] Cause-related marketing is not part of online marketing. Nevertheless, it often includes online marketing tools such as linked websites (like for example the movie *Igor* with Malaria association.

[81] In the sample, the horror films were only 2, so this assumption is based only on the film *Quarantine*, but according to the theory, it is likely to be true for the category in general.

subscribed between the boundaries of the category more the marketing is likely to be easy and effective[82].

In order to draw some final recommendations it is useful to comment two of the most significant movies of the sample, both champions of excellence. The first one is the Warner Bros' *The Dark Knight*, which had the first "US Opening Weekend of All Time[83]", ranking at the second place[84] in the "US All Time Box Office" and at the fourth place in the "Worldwide All Time Box Office[85]". But the latest movie of the Batman franchise is a champion not only with the box office and the critics' reviews[86], but it has also deployed one of the greatest online marketing campaigns of all time: the main vehicle has been the alternative reality game developed by 42Entertainment[87] and started on May 2007 with the website *ibelieveinharveydent.com*, a game that developed along the 15 months prior to the release of the film in theatres and dragged in million of fans using the Web with the support of offline events. The A.R.G. combined with other marketing tools (such as an impressive mobile marketing campaign and a lot of co-branding initiatives) in a long, persistent and powerful marketing campaign that rumors[88] state has cost more than $100 million[89] (that would be more than the half of the production budget, estimated at $185,000,000).

---

[82] This comment considers the film only from a marketing perspective, ignoring any consequences about the quality and value of the movie.

[83] It opened on 2008 July 18 with $158,411,483, all data from http://www.imdb.com.

[84] With a US box office at the 31 October 2008 of $528,213,279.

[85] With a Worldwide box office at the 6 November 2008 of $992,213,279.

[86] It gained 94% at rottentomatoes.com and 9.1 at imdb.com.

[87] http://www.42entertainment.com.

[88] For example this amount is cited in the article *"Marketing the Dark Knight: A Viral Revolution"*, posted on *http://www.filmschoolrejects.com/news/marketing-the-dark-knight-a-viral-revolution.php*.

[89] It is indeed important to point out that the film has received a further boost of awareness with the sudden death on January 2008 of Heath Ledger, the young actor that played the Joker.

The second film of the sample that deserves a particular consideration is *Fireproof*, a drama about the marriage's troubles of a couple, produced with a budget of $500,000[90]. This movie didn't dispose of any famous talent or contents that could be easily used in the marketing campaign, and nevertheless achieved an impressive box office of over 26 million of dollars[91]. The key of success was the engagement of the Christian community (primary audience of the film[92]) through the official website's design as a portal of information about the movie and the values behind it; moreover the website asked to the community to help promoting the film, providing movie related material for helping to spread the buzz.

The Dark Knight and *Fireproof* are different in almost everything, but they have both achieved a great box office result (obviously considering the size of the budget) and promoted through a superior online marketing campaign. If compared, the two online strategies present similarities that could be an explanation of their success and effectiveness:

- Both films have a specific and defined core audience, target of the first marketing wave (*Fireproof*: Christian married couple; *The Dark Knight*: comics' geeks)
- Both the online marketing campaigns started a long time before the release of the film in theatres (*Fireproof*: 11 months, *The Dark Knight*: 15 months[93]);
- Each campaign focused on a main tool that worked as vehicle for the other marketing efforts (*Fireproof*: blog and website; *The Dark Knight*: A.R.G.);
- The selected online marketing tool was relevant with the film's contents and with the core audience (*Fireproof*: a blog to target couples and talk about marriage; *The Dark Knight*: an alternative reality games to engage comics' geeks);
- Both of the online marketing campaigns relied on the core audience for spreading the buzz to the other segments of population (*Fireproof*: the official websites of-

---

[90] The budget is so reduced thanks to the volunteer efforts and Christian communities donations, like cited on *imdb.com* (http://pro.imdb.com/news/ni0592073/).

[91] $26,114,966 on October 31 2008

[92] Actually the primary target of audience is Christian married couples.

[93] The *Fireproof*'s Blog started on November 1, 2007 and the film released on September 26, 2008; *The Dark Knight*'s website was launched on May 2007 and the film released on July 18, 2008.

fered banners and other downloads to spread the word online and also explained how to request the film on local theatres; *The Dark Knight*: the extension and deepness of the game scattered the enthusiasm of the fans, that spread the buzz all over the Internet and attracted also the media attention, granting a worldwide media coverage of the events).

These common factors between the two online marketing strategies help to define three overall principles that could be used as guidelines in designing an effective film online marketing campaign: *consistency, early-seeding* and *audience empowerment.* The *consistency* of an online marketing campaign involves the relationships between the film's contents, the choice of marketing tools and the targeted audience:

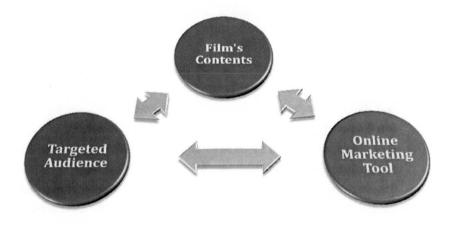

Figure 39 - The consistency of an online marketing campaign

It is necessary indeed to have relevance between the contents of the film, the segment of audience targeted (that is usually defined as the audience that will more likely watch the movie) and the online marketing tools implemented in the campaign to target that audience. It is anyway useful to point out that some tools are necessary apart from this guideline, like for example be listed in the organic search results pages or having a good official website. Examples of consistency besides *The Dark Knight* (comic-based action film – comics' geeks – alternative reality game) and *Fireproof* (marriage troubles' drama – Christian married couples – community website and blog) could be *Quarantine* ("zombies" horror movie – teenagers – online videogames and social networks presence), *Wall-E* (animation film about a small robot – kids and children – online games/activities, consumer products and fast foods promoting partnerships) and *College* (well, college comedy – college teenagers – video contest, Facebook page and application, online games). For that concerns the consistency, there are two level of decision that requires a particular attention: the first one is choosing the right audience for the film, that regards the targeting strategy and the analysis of the product, topics that go beyond this analysis. The second level involves the choice of the right online marketing tool for targeting the selected audience or for promoting the film's contents: some tools are more addressed to specific segments of audience or to promote certain genres of film, and selecting an inappropriate one could cause the ineffectiveness of the marketing. It is also true that with a work of creativity each tool could be modeled on the needs of the scenario: even if Advergaming is usually conceived to target young males, women-targeted films like *Sex and the City*[94] and *The Sisterhood of the Traveling Pants 2*[95] used on their official websites personality quizzes related to the films contents targeted to women.

The second principle of an online marketing strategy is the *early-seeding*, which simply means that the online campaign, or at least the first efforts, should start a long time before the release of the movie in theatres. Studios can espouse two different lines of action once a film is announced[96]: they just can let rumors and unofficial news flourish thanks to the pure interest of fans or they can coordinate and stimulate the fans through first efforts of online marketing, like posting a first draft of the Official Website or publishing a production blog. It is an extremely powerful way to seed the fans with firsthand news and material about their favorite film, creating, feeding and growing the core audience of the film. This happens very frequently with comics' based and sci-fi films,

[94] http://www.sexandthecitymovie.com

[95] http://sisterhoodofthetravelingpants2.warnerbros.com/guys.html

[96] That usually happens when the studio approve the project, and the shootings have still to start.

like with *The Dark Knight* or *Iron Man*, and it is also happening for some upcoming film of 2009: *Terminator Salvation*, fourth installment of the Terminator franchise, will be released on May 22, 2009[97] and one year before, only few days after the shootings started, Warner Bros' posted the production blog[98] written by the director McG, keeping updated the fans about the development of the movie. An even more strong application of this principle comes with another Warner Bros' flick, Watchmen, based on a graphic novel and due for March 2009: the blog was posted on July 2007 when the director Zack Snyder presented the idea of the film, even before the production actually started[99], and it offers news, comments of the filmmakers and also video journals following the shootings on the movie set.

The last principle represents a consequence of the previous ones: after having achieved a *consistence* among contents-audience-tool and started to grow a core audience through an *early-seeding* online campaign, a further step is represented by the *Audience Empowerment*, which means that studios should encourage movie fans to spread the buzz and market the film. Actually the rise of Internet caused to companies an effective loss of control of their brands, which corporate images are promoted or denigrated by Internet users, which through this medium can manifest without limits their opinions and ideas, in what is defined the Internet Democracy. Movie studios have a choice: recognizes this loss of control and helping fans to promote their favorite films or simply ignoring them and keep doing the old fashioned marketing through one-way advertising tools. Even if the most part of them choose the second path, some of the films in the analyzed sample showed an opposite trend of audience empowerment, which could be realized in several different ways, like providing banners and badges to be posted on personal websites (like for *Fireproof* and *Indiana Jones and the Kingdom of the Crystal Skull*), involving the audience in user-generated contest (like for *Get Smart* and *Hamlet 2*) or in advanced experiences like the alternative reality games (like for *The Dark Knight* and *Hellboy II: the Golden Army*).

---

[97] All dates from IMDb.com.

[98] http://rss.warnerbros.com/terminatorsalvation/

[99] Production of *Watchmen* officially started on September 27, 2007, from http://IMDb.com.

Effective Online
Marketing Campaign

Figure 40 - The three principles for an effective online marketing campaign

Films are extremely complex products: placed on the edge between art and industry (Salvemini, 1992), each of them is the unique result of a combination of several different factors. This complexity causes a substantial unpredictability of box office results, which are influenced also by factors beyond the film per se. Among the factors actually under the control of production houses, marketing plays the important rule of providing information to the audience, in the tentative of persuading it to watch the film in theatres. There are several ways by which marketing tries to achieve its goals, but one in particular has acquired in the last few years a particular influence on the audience: online marketing. This new marketing on the Internet is constantly evolving with new technologies and applications, and also the slow changing Hollywood studios have started to recognize the power of the Web, with the exploration of new online marketing tools to reach the moviegoers on the Internet.

The strong diffusion of online marketing in film promotion finds justification in its capacity to influence the moviegoing decision, an assumption that has been tried to verify through the analysis of the online marketing campaigns in a sample of 66 films released in the U.S. theatres. By means of an online marketing scorecard, the campaigns' scores have been correlated with different variables, finding results that confirmed the positive correlation of the scores with the first weekend's box office, the first three weeks' box office and also with the production budget. A qualitative introspection into the most significant cases has then helped in providing three guidelines for a successful online marketing campaign, that are the *consistency*, the *early-seeding* and the *audience empowerment*.

In conclusion, it is possible to state that the online marketing campaign can have a positive influence on the box office results; at the same time, its quality is in someway influenced by the production budget invested in the film. The variance in the characteristics of films does not allow any specific recommendations about which online marketing tool deploy: it is anyway possible to suggest with a good certainty three principles that could be followed for designing an effective online marketing campaign. This consists in finding the appropriate tools for the targeted segment of audience, start the online efforts with great advance and share with the audience the task of promoting the film. Movie marketing on the Internet does not require any advanced technical skills either substantial financial resources or long experience, but what is necessary are the same ingredients needed to shoot a good film: great ideas and a lot of creativity.

Exhibit 1 – The construction of the Scorecard - Methodology

Introduction to the Scorecard

The scorecard is built combining the nine categories of online marketing tools, each of them analyzed in their components. Each single characteristic is evaluated using a discrete scale of values from 0 to 7 (0,1,2,3,4,5,6,7). Sometimes instead of a numeric evaluation has been used a qualitative judgement, from *weak* to *excellent* (*weak, fair, good, excellent*)[100], that has been successively converted in a numeric value utilizing the following conversion chart:

Qualitative Judgement	Points
Not Available	0
Weak	1
Fair	3
Good	5
Excellent	7

[100] The complete online marketing scorecard will be presented on Exhibit 2: the qualitative judgments are abbreviated with the first capital letter; for reasons of format, the chart in the Exhibit 2 excludes the data that were not used for computing the final score.

Each characteristic is then weighted applying a percentage weight, in order to obtain a unique score for each of the tool. The same will apply for the final score, when the score of each tool will be weighted using a percentage weight.

The evaluation of each tool has required specific assumptions that are described below.

1. Official Website Score

- The *official website* per se accounts for the 70% of the final score (*Look* and *Content* account 50% each for the website score);
- *UGC* and *Community Acknowledgement* accounts 15% each of the final score;
- The equation to obtain the total score of *Official Website*, *UGC* and *Community Acknowledgement* is the following:
    - [(*look* x 50% + *content* x 50%)x 70% + *UGC* x 15% + *C.A.* x 15%]
- The number of URLs linked to the official website is a consequence of the previous components of the official website, so the points will be added to the previous equation:
    - The maximum number of links of all the sample of films analyzed is 5'693 that corresponds to 7 points: the other scores are assigned as a consequence, using a 0-7 scale (5693 : 7 = n°links : X)
- The final score of the OFFICIAL WEBSITE is composed by:
    - 60% from the qualitative score;
    - 40% from the quantitative score (the URLs).
- The reasons why the qualitative score accounts more than the quantitative one is that the URLs search results may not be directly correlated to the quality of the official websites and may be influenced by other factors. The qualitative analysis instead is conducted on each components of the website, even if not supported by numbers

- *MySpace*: the points of the *MySpace* presence are composed by 70% from the qualitative judgement of the page content and by 30% from the number of friends. The reason of this reduced weight of the quantitative data is that film pages are online from different dates, so the number of friends may be influenced by the effective days that these pages are online: some of them are older than others, making this data not suitable for a stronger weight.
  - The number of friends are converted in a 0-7 scale: the maximum point (7) is assigned to the highest number of friends (43640), and the others are obtained through the equation $43640 : 7 = n°friends : X$
- *Facebook*
  - *Page*: same speech of the *MySpace* page, 70% of the score from the qualitative judgement of the page content, 30% from the number of friends; the page accounts for the 50% of the Facebook final score, since it is the main tool used to promote a film on Facebook. The range of friends varies from the maximum of 912741 for *The Dark Knight* to the minimum of 61 for *The Brideshead Revisited*. This top extreme will not be considerate in the scale, in order to normalize the score. So 7 points will be assigned to 205270 of *Iron Man* and the others using the equation $205270 : 7 = friends : X$. *The Dark Knight* will receive 7 points.
  - *Applications*: besides the qualitative judgement on the application content, there would be a quantitative indicator, which is the monthly users of the application: unfortunately some of the applications are not stand-alone, but are simply features integrated in pre-existing applications, making impossible to determine their number of users. So the score will be only obtained from the qualitative judgement. Moreover, to simplify the evaluation, it will be not take into consideration if the application is new or just an integration of a pre-existing one. The first application has an importance of 40%, while the second one (if present) accounts for 10%. This because the efforts of the marketers should focus in publishing a valuable application, preferring the quality to the quantity.

- *Gift:* the presence of Facebook gifts is not relevant to the final scorecard: the reason is that there are no criteria to evaluate this tool, neither quantitative or qualitative.
- *Others:* the presence in other social network websites will be evaluated only from a qualitative judgement of the content, since the quantitative indicators (like the number of friends) are not comparable from one network to another, and also in some of them this data are not available.

- Since *MySpace* and *Facebook* are the 2 main social network websites of the Web, their presence account for 40% each one, while each of the *Others* networks account for 10% each one

3. Syndicated Content Score

- Between *blogs* and *podcasts*, *blogs* are the ones more common in the movie marketing and also more widespread among the online community. For this reasons, *blogs* account for the 70% of the final score and *podcasts* for 30%.
- *Blog*
  - *Content:* the qualitative judgement of the content is on a scale 0-7 and it accounts for the 40% of the final score.
  - *N°posts* : the number of posts will be converted in a scale 0-7: the top extreme (115 posts for *Fireproof*) will not be used in the scale conversion, in order to normalize the score. The top used for reference will be 32 for *X-Files: I want to believe*, that will have 7 points. The others will be calculated with the equation
  - $32 : 7 = $ n°posts $: X$. *Fireproof* will receive 7 points. *N° posts* will account for 30% of the final score.
  - *Time Extension:* the number of months will be converted in a 0-7 scale. The top number of months is 12 for *Blindness* that will have 7 points, the others will be calculated using the equations $12 : 7 = $ n°months $: X$. *Time Extension* will account for 30% of the final score.

110

- The *Updates Frequency* and the *Sharing Options* will be not taken into account for the evaluation.

- *Podcast*
  - *Content*: the qualitative evaluation of the podcast is converted into a 0-7 scale. The content account for 50% of the final podcast score.
  - *N°posts*: since in the sample of observations there are only 4 podcasts (on a group of 66 films analyzed), these have a number of posts of 3, 4 and 16. 7 points will be assigned to the podcast with 16 posts (*Get Smart*), 3 points to the podcast with 4 posts (*Wall-E*), 1 point to the podcast with 3 posts (*Kung Fu Panda, X-Files I Want To Believe*). The n°posts account for 50% of the final *podcast* score.
  - *Updates Frequency* will be not taken into account for the final *podcast* score.

4. Mobile Marketing Score

- *Downloads*: mobile *downloads* are the main tools of promoting films on mobile platforms, since they can be used for all kind of films. The weight of this category on the mobile scorecard is of 60%.
- *N° of categories*: the possible categories of downloads are ringtones (or voice-tones), wallpapers, screensavers and videos, for a total of 4 categories. The points will be assigned with 7 points to the presence of all 4 categories, 5 points to 3 categories, 3 points to 2 categories, 1 point to 1 category. This feature account for 50% of the *Downloads* points
- *Quantity*: this feature accounts for 50% of the *Downloads* score. The number of downloads available is converted through this table:

N° of downloads	Points
1 to 5	1
6 to 10	2
11 to 20	3
21 to 30	5
>31	7

- *Mobile Game*: the qualitative judgement of the content of the mobile game is converted into a 0-7 scale (0 if not present). The weight of the mobile game on the final mobile score cannot be superior to the other categories, since not all the films has content suitable for a mobile game, but only certain genre. The weight is determined on 10%.
- *Mobile Website*: the presence of a mobile-friendly version of the official film website is an important feature that helps movie marketing to step into the mobile platforms. The weight on the final scorecard is of 20%. The presence of a mobile website is rewarded with 7 points, the absence with 0.
- *Other*: if any other mobile marketing tool is present, this will be evaluated converting the qualitative judgement into a 0-7 scale. The weight is of 10% (since there are very few films that use further mobile marketing tools).

5. Advergaming Score

- *Alternative Reality Game*: of all the films analyzed, only 2 have utilized ARGs (*The Dark Knight, Hellboy II*). Since *The Dark Knight*'s ARG has used 3 different media over a period of 15 months, its evaluation is *excellent*, earning 7 points. The *Hellboy II*'s one use only the Web, over a period of three months, obtaining an evaluation of *fair* (3 points). Even if not common, ARGs accounts for the 20% of the final score, due to their strong contribution to the marketing campaign.

- *Web-based games*: this is the most important advergaming tool used in movie marketing. For this reasons, web-based games accounts for the 80% of the final score.

  - *Relevance*: the qualitative judgement on the relevance of the games is converted on a 0-7 scale. The relevance of the web-game with the film content counts for the 70% of the score, since it is considered more important having few games that are relevant with the film content that a lot of games created just to fill the official website;

  - *Quantity*: the number of games accounts for the 30% of the final score, and is converted on points using the following conversion chart:

Number of Web-based games	Points
0	0
1	2
2	3
3	4
4-5	5
6-10	6
>10	7

- *In-Game Advertising*: even if this type of advertising is extremely effective, of the universe of 66 films observed only 1 (*Tropic Thunder*) has used this tool. For this reason, this category will not be considered into the final score.

- Spin-off videogame: not all the films are suitable for a conversion into a video-game. Besides, the decision for a spin-off videogame is not directly managed by the marketers of the films, even if the launch of a videogame could help to spread the buzz around the movie. For this reasons, the presence of a spin-off videogame will not be considered for the final score.

6. Cross Brand Marketing

- As discussed in the dedicated paragraph, the approach to promotional partners in film could either be quantitative or qualitative. The quantitative approach suggests involving in the film promotions as many partners as possible, while the qualitative approach is for a more selected range of partners that fits with the core audience of the film. The main goal of movie marketing is reaching the target audience with the promotional message, so adopting a qualitative approach seems to be more appropriate for that purpose. For this reason the relevance of the partners will account more than the quantity of the partners, which means 50% of relevance versus 35% of the n° *of partners.*
- *N° of partners*: the number of partners will be converted in points using the following conversion chart

Number of Partners	Points
1	1
2-3	2
4-6	3
7-9	4
10-12	5

13-15	6
>16	7

- *Relevance*: the qualitative judgement on the relevance of the promotional partner will be converted in a 0-7 scale. The weight of the relevance on the final score is of 50%.
- *N° of tools categories*: on the 66 films analyzed, the maximum number of online marketing tools implemented by promotional partners is 7 (for *The Dark Knight*). For each type of tool implemented will be assigned a point: 7 tools = 7 points, 6 tools = 6 points and so on. Even if the deployment of a wide range of different tools is a sign of a strong support, the lack of a judgement for each of the tool deployed does not allow a stronger weight of this characteristic, that is of 15%

7. Viral Marketing Score

- *Measuring the buzz*: even if the number of results of the blog searches (both the Google and the Technorati ones) are useful to indicate the dimension of the buzz around the film, there are too many factors that may distort the results. Some films' titles are very common words and is almost impossible to discriminate. For these reasons, the search results will be not be taken into consideration for the viral marketing score.
- *Other*: the presence of other tools of viral marketing is evaluated converting the existing qualitative judgement into a 0-7 scale. The weight on the viral marketing score is of 50%.
- *Viral Message*: the viral message is often the main tool of viral marketing implemented in movie marketing campaigns and accounts for the 50% of the total score.
  - *N° of sharing options*: the viral message has the goal to be spread around, so it should provide to the user a lot of sharing options. Unfortunately, on

the 17 films that use viral messages, only one provides more than 3 sharing options. It accounts for the 40% of the *viral message* score. The conversion chart is the following:

Number of Sharing Options	Points
1	1
2	2
3	3
4-6	4
7-9	5
10-13	6
>13	7

- o *Content Evaluation*: the qualitative judgement of the content will be converted in a 0-7 scale, and it will weight for the 60% of the *viral message* score.

8. Search Engine Marketing Score

- Of all the 66 films observed, only one has used *Google Ads* (the Disney's *Wall-E*), so they will not take into consideration for the score.

- For what concerns the *organic search results*, the points will be assigned to strengthen the importance of being in the top 5 results of the organic research:

Ranking	Points
1st	7
2nd	5
3rd	4
5th	2
5th-10th	1
>10th	0

9. Widget Marketing Score

- *Content Evaluation*: the qualitative evaluation of the content will be converted in a 0-7 scale. The weight on the *widget marketing* score is of 50%.
- *N° of sharing options*:: the goal of the widget is to be posted on more websites as possible, so having a great number of sharing options is very important. The weight on the widget marketing score is of 50%. The conversion chart between the number of sharing options and the points is the following:

N° of sharing options	Points
>30	7
25-30	6
20-25	5
15-20	4
10-15	3
5-10	2
<5	1

10. The construction of the final score

In the end, each film is analyzed according to nine main categories of tools: official website, social networking websites, syndicated content, mobile marketing, advergaming, cross brand marketing, viral marketing, search engine marketing and widget marketing.

In order to summarize all the different scores for each category in a unique indicator that evaluates the overall online marketing strategy of the film, it is necessary to assign a weight for each category. But how is possible to distribute an appropriate weight to each online marketing tool? Which one could be regarded as more effective?

First of all, this online marketing scorecard should be designed to be applied to all genres of films, without any kind of distinction: a first criterion that could be applied to the different tools is indeed the suitability of the tool to all kind of films. This leads to divide the nine tools into two groups: the tools that can be used to market all genres of films and the tools that can't. The last group will include the following tools:

- *Cross Brand Marketing*: the content of certain type of films are not suitable to be partnered with brands. It would be dangerous or counterproductive for brands to associate their image with films with mature content such as violence, sex, death and so on: for example rarely horror films have promotional partners. A curious exceptions happened for the release of the Steven Spielberg's *War of the Worlds*, when the hi-tech company Hitachi partnered for a worldwide cross promotion: the results of the partnership were pretty disappointing for the brand, probably for the strong negative content of the movie, that was the end of the world and a global war (Schiller, 2005);
- *Advergaming*: not all the genre of films can be easily converted into games. Drama movies and documentary for example, due also to their adult contents, do not have contents that are suitable to be "played", neither their audience probably consists in gamers;
- *Viral Marketing*: even if almost everything could go "viral", there are without any doubt certain films which content is more willing to be used in a viral marketing campaign. Horrors, comedies, thrillers and sci-fi have many more possibilities to be promoted through a viral campaign than other genre of films.

SUITABLE	NOT SUITABLE
Official Website	Cross Brand Marketing
Search Engine Marketing	Advergaming
Social Networking Websites	Viral Marketing
Mobile Marketing	
Widget Marketing	
Syndicated Content	

The tools that are "suitable" will have a greater weight than the "non suitable" ones. It is important anyway to point up that an online marketing tool that has been classified as "non suitable" does not necessarily mean that can't be applied at all to certain genre of films: all tools can be applied to all kind of movies, just some tools are more incline to be generic than others. This is a distinction applied with the purpose to differentiate the tools and making easier to assign them different weights.

Of the six categories that have been classified as "suitable", a further classification could be applied according to the popularity of the tool: some tools are regarded as standards of any online marketing strategy, like the basement on which building more advanced strategies. The two most common used online marketing tools (on all the categories analyzed) are the Official Website and the Search Engine Marketing, which are implemented respectively by the 98.48% and the 95.45% of the films. Of this two, the Official Website can be regarded as the more standard and common tool of online marketing, as well as the "field" of application of the Search Engine Marketing, which involves also the optimization of websites in order to improve their ranking in the search engine result pages. For these reasons, the Official Website will have a greater weight than the S.E.M., and both will have a greater weight than the other four categories of the "suitable" group.

Before assigning the different weights, an exception to the above described rules has to be applied for the Mobile Marketing category. Even if it is classified as an online marketing tool, it is on the border between the Internet and the Mobile media: almost all of the mobile content comes from Internet websites, where are available all kind of downloads to be displayed on mobile cellphones. From the other hand, the content per-se is "consumed" not on the Internet but on mobile devices. For these reasons, mobile marketing is at the border of online marketing and, beyond its belonging to the "suitable" group, it will have the smaller weight of all the categories.

The final score will belong in a scale from 0 to 7, in order to maintain a certain consistency all over the scorecard. The weights will be in percentages (%), and assigned according to the following chart, where the categories are ranked according to the greater weight:

Categories	Weight Percentage
Official Website	16%
Search Engine Marketing	14%
Widget Marketing Social Networking Websites Syndicated Content	12%
Cross Brand Marketing Viral Marketing Advergaming	9%
Mobile Marketing	7%

Exhibit 2 – The Online Marketing Scorecard

Category	Metric	The Dark Knight	Pineapple express	The Mummy: Tomb of the Dragon Emperor	The Sisterhood of the Traveling Pants 2	Step Brothers	Mamma Mia!	Journey to the Center of the Earth
WIDGET MARKETING	Content evaluation / location	O	F	W	W	O	O	O
	N sharing contacts	29	29	1	1	24	29 (12)	29
SEM – GOOGLE	Ranking	1st	2nd	1st	13th	1st	1st	1st
VIRAL MARKETING – Other viral	Evaluation	E					F	O
Viral message	Content evaluation	E				F	E	W
	N of sharing options	3			1	3	1	
CROSS BRAND MARKETING	N of tools / category	O 7		O 4	O 3		O 3	O 2
	Relevance	O		F	F		O	O
	N partners	10	0	8	17	0	7	7
ADVERGAMING – Alternative reality games	Time extension	15 months						
	Media used	fake websites, mobiles, real life events						
Web-based games	Relevance	E	F	E	O	F	O	E
	Quantity	1	1	1	2	2	3	4
MOBILE MARKETING – Other	Evaluation	E					O	
	Description	iPhone Application "Jokerize Yourself"					mobile content widget application	
Mobile site	Presence	yes	no	no	no	no	no	no
Mobile game	Relevance	E		E				
	Downloads quantity	57	12	28	13			
	N of categories	4	1	2	2			
SYNDICATED CONTENT – Podcasts	N posts / content							
Blogs	Time extension		11 months					3 months
	N posts / content		O 10					F 21
SOCIAL NETWORKING WEBSITES – Facebook	App content / N of apps	E, 1			0	F, 1	F W, 2	
	N friends	900,205	84,844	4,335	25,418	42,880	66,961	
	Page content	E	O	W	O	E	W	
Myspace	N friends	40,505	16,566	3,896	13,854			
	Page content	O	E	O	E			
OFFICIAL WEBSITE – References	Technorati / URL search	5,580	354	682	223	232	1,198	401
Community acknowledgement	Evaluation / description						O movie fans website	
UGC	Description	O fan art		F fan art				
Official website	Look	E	F	E	F	O	E	O
	Content	O	O	O	O	O	E	O

Hancock	E			...6	E	O	E F	2	E F	O	O	3rd	4 E		no	E	w 4	w 4			E F	O 3rd	F
Wall-E	E			2.735	E 23.465	O 177.635	E	1 w			O 1 2		E 11		yes	E 44	4				1st	G 1st	G 29
Swing Vote	F	w		77		w 120	w				O		E 3		no						13th	O	O
Space Chimps	G	O		190		w 352					G 6 5		E 3		no						1st	E 1st	E
X-Files: I Want To Believe	E	F	community chat, links O	1.619		F 13.616	E			F 3 2 2 months		0		0		no		2 5				1st	69 E
Hellboy II: The Golden Army	E	E	web ring, wiki, message board E	1.717	O	w 3.310	1	fan art G			w 5 1	4 websites months	F 1		yes	E 3 8					1st	F F	29 F
Brideshead revisited	F	F		113		w 41					0		0		no						>5 0th		
Wanted	E	E		1.539	O 12.494	O 89.178	1 E				G 3 2		E 3	mobile sweepstake F	no	E					3rd	E 3rd	E
Get Smart	E	E	UGC contest E	837	E 5.044	E 29.122	1 F		Bebo E		O 1 4		F 1		yes	E 20	O 16				2nd	2nd	
Kung Fu Panda	E	E		1.866		O 173.631	1 G		myYearBook.com E		G 6 8		E 6		no	G	w 3				1st	E 1st	G 29
Iron Man	F	E	fan art O	3.316	E 42.610	F 200.930					O 8		0		no	O 3 9					1st	E 1st	E 29
Tell No One	w	E		26							0		0		no						2nd	2nd	
The Incredible Hulk	E	O	fan art O	1.790	E 13.752	w 4.764	1 E				O 1 1		E 1	SMS campaign F	no	F					1st	E 1st	G 29
Bottle Shock	G	O		255		F 372					0		0		no						1st	1st	
Man On Wire	w	w		326		w 525					0		0		no						1st	1st	

Title	Code		N					Platform	Period			no/yes								Rank
Kit Kittredge: An American Girl	O O		180		W 149				w 1 0 3 months			no		2 F		1 E					2n d
Indiana Jones and the Kingdom of the Crystal Skull	E O		5.693	E 43.640	O 130.254	3 E				2 10 E		no		0		9 F 3			1 E	29 E	1s t
Beer for My Horses	W W		27									no		0		0					1s t
Tropic Thunder	O E		1.103	G 14.199	E 33.655	1 E				3 14 E		no		2 G		0	2 G		2 O	23 E	1s t
Star Wars: The Clone Wars	O O		481		W 1.390							no		3 E		4 W				64 E	1s t
Mirrors	O F		266		W 1.390					1 3		no		0		0					2n d
Vicky Cristina Barcelona	W W		308		W 6.865		F					no		0		2 O 1					1s t
Henry Poole Is Here	W W	UGC contest G	70	W 7.424	W 123							no		0		0					2n d
The House Bunny	F F	LikeMe.net O	174	O 12.689	O 28.976					2 21 E		no		3 O		2 O 2	1 W		2 G		1s t
Death Race	O O		318		W 9.575					2		no		1 E		0	21 E				2n d
The Longshots	W W		35									no		0		0					2n d
The Rocker	F O	YouTube Channel F	105	E 9.517	O 2.003		G			2 5		no		2 E		4 O 2					1s t
Harriet 2	O F	Forum F	22		W 1.939				w 3 1 month			no		0		2 F 2					2n d
Babylon A.D.	W F	UGC contest E	226	O 5.042	W 1.204				w 2 0 2 months			no		1 O		0	0			10 W	1s t
Traitor	O E		119	O 251	F 232		O					no		4 E		0					2n d

Movie														Rank	
Disaster Movie	F	F		136		F 2.205				no		1 F	0		1st	
College	F	E	UOC contest E	50	E 2.161	G 1.332	breako.com E			no		2 E	2 E 1	2 G	3rd	24 E
Bangkok Dangerous	F	G		91	G 6	W 425				no		3 E	0		3rd	
Burn After Reading	F	F		69		F 1.967 1 F			E 1 4	no		1 W	0		3rd	11 E
The Family That Prays	F	F								no		1 F	0		2nd	
Righteous Kill	G	F		321		W 945		F 3 0 2 months	E 3 9	no		2 G	1 W		1st	29 G
The Women	F	W		279		W 99				no		0	3 G	3 E	1st	58 F
Lakeview Terrace	W	F		88		F 588				no		1 F	0		2nd	
My Best Friend's Girl	F	F	UOC contest	107		W 338 1 F				no		0	1 W	2 G	1st	1 W
Igor	G	G		137	G 4.131	F 866 1 W	bebo.com G twitter.com G			no		0	18 1	3 E	3rd	
Ghost Town	F	F		192		W 187				no		0	0		2nd	
Eagle Eye	F	F		588		G 8.881 1 E				yes — mobile marketing campaign E	E	2 E	0		2nd	
Nights in Rodanthe	W	W		153						no		0	10 W		2nd	
Fireproof	E	F	community website G	1.296		W 2.394		E 1 15 11		no		1 E	8 E 1		1st	2 E
Miracle at St. Anna	W	F		136		W 264				no		0	0		1st	

Title																	
Choke	O E			236		W 416		G 7 / 2 months		no	0		1 G 1	2 E		2nd	8 F
The Duchess	F F			203		F 436				no	0		2 F 2			1st	
Beverly Hills Chihuahua	O G			236						no	1 F		0	1 E E	E	1st	
Nick and Norah's Infinite Playlist	F E		E 13,388	180		E 13,019			2 11	no	0		5 G 2	1	E	2nd	21 E
Appaloosa	F F			22					2 8	no	0		1 W 0			3rd	
An American Carol	F F		W 8,611	266		F 2,857	Facebook Profile MySpace Profile W			no	0		2 F 1	1 W	E	4th	
Religulous	W F			339		W 1,547			3 10	no	0		0		E	1st	
Flash of Genus	F G			114		W 127				no	0		0			2nd	29 G
Blindness	F E			400		W 340 2 E F		E 5 / 12 months		no	0		0	1 E		2nd	
How to Lose Friends & Alienate People	O O			62		E 335	twitter.com G	E 7 / 3 months		no	0		0		G	2nd	23 E
Quarantine	F E		E 3,111	129		O 3,419	bebo.com F twitter.com F			no	1 G		4 W 2	1	G	2nd	17 G
Body Of Lies	F F			102		W 775				no	1 E		0		G	1st	
The Express	O F			87		W 145				no	0		2 E 0			2nd	29 G
City of Ember			W 127	221		W 151		E 0 / 3 months		no	2 E		0	E	E	1st	29 G

Exhibit 3 – The Release Weekend's Box Office Ranking & Distribution Chart

Position	Film	Release Weekend's Box Office	Official Website 16%	Social Network Websites 12%	Syndicated Content 12%	Mobile Mktg 7%	Adverga ming 9%	Cross Brand Mktg 9%	Viral Mktg 9%	SEM 14%	Widget Mktg 12%	TOTAL SCORE
1	The Dark Knight	158.411.483	5,52	4,70	0,00	7,0	5,80	5,3	6,2	7	3,5	4,89
2	Indiana Jones and the Kingdom of the Crystal Skull	126.917.373	5,04	4,77	0,00	2,2	0,00	3,35	0,0	7	6,5	3,59
3	Iron Man	102.118.668	4,20	3,62	0,00	2,6	0,00	5,8	3,5	7	6,5	3,89
4	Wall-E	63.087.526	4,44	2,57	0,60	6,3	5,60	5	2,5	7	5,5	4,35
5	Hancock	62.603.879	2,34	2,32	0,00	0,7	5,12	0	2,5	4	4,5	2,49
6	Kung Fu Panda	60.239.130	4,12	2,56	0,30	3,1	5,36	5,85	0,0	7	5,5	3,87
7	The Incredible Hulk	55.414.050	4,65	2,38	0,00	0,6	4,40	4,7	0,0	7	5,5	3,53
8	Wanted	50.927.085	4,00	3,66	0,00	1,0	4,88	3,5	3,5	4	0	2,78
9	The Mummy: Tomb of the Dragon Emperor	40.457.770	3,51	0,15	3,21	3,1	4,40	3,5	0,0	7	1	2,99
10	Get Smart	38.683.480	3,98	3,98	1,80	2,1	2,16	5,2	1,1	5	0	2,94
11	Hellboy II: The Golden Army	34.539.115	5,32	1,63	0,00	4,2	2,76	1,7	3,5	7	4,5	3,58
12	Step Brothers	30.940.732	2,54	3,46	0,00	2,3	2,40	0	4,2	7	5	3,16
13	Beverly Hills Chihuahua	29.300.465	2,54	0,00	0,00	1,8	2,16	0	5,8	7	0	2,23
14	Eagle Eye	29.150.721	1,69	1,85	0,00	2,8	4,64	0	0,0	5	0	1,81
15	Mamma Mia!	27.751.240	3,91	0,81	0,00	0,0	3,76	4,2	0,5	7	5,5	3,12
16	Tropic Thunder	25.812.796	2,86	3,85	0,00	2,4	3,52	0	5,4	7	6	3,59
17	Pineapple express	23.245.025	2,09	3,15	0,00	1,2	2,16	0	0,0	5	4,5	2,23
18	Journey to the Center of the Earth	21.018.141	2,60	0,00	2,17	0,0	5,12	4,2	2,5	7	5,5	3,38

Po siti on	Film	Release Weekend's Box Office	Official Website	Social Network Websites	Syndica ted Content	Mobile Mktg	Adverga ming	Cross Brand Mktg	Viral Mktg	SEM	Widg et Mktg	TOTAL SCORE
19	Bum After Reading	19.128.001	1,50	2,31	0,00	0,6	1,04	0	0,0	4	5	1,81
20	The Family That Preys	17.381.218	1,47	0,00	0,00	0,0	2,16	0	0,5	5	0	1,17
21	Righteous Kill	16.288.361	2,08	0,14	0,00	2,1	3,52	1	0,0	7	5,5	2,54
22	Lakeview Terrace	15.004.672	1,01	0,42	0,00	0,0	2,16	0	0,0	5	0	1,11
23	Star Wars: The Clone Wars	14.611.273	3,12	0,00	0,00	0,0	4,88	1,55	0,0	7	7	2,90
24	The House Bunny	14.533.702	1,53	2,91	0,00	2,4	3,76	3,5	0,5	7	0	2,44
25	Quarantine	14.211.321	2,50	3,33	0,00	0,0	4,40	1,85	2,5	7	4,5	3,11
26	Nights in Rodanthe	13.418.454	0,55	0,00	0,00	0,0	0,00	2,7	0,0	5	0	1,03
27	Body Of Lies	12.834.416	1,51	0,14	0,00	0,0	0,00	0	0,0	7	0	1,24
28	Death Race	12.621.090	2,57	0,18	0,00	1,6	4,40	0	3,5	5	0	1,96
29	Babylon A.D	11.541.571	1,06	1,64	1,44	0,0	3,28	0	0,0	7	2	2,06
30	Nick and Norah's Infinite Playlist	11.311.751	2,52	3,23	0,00	1,5	0,00	3,85	0,0	5	6	2,66
31	Mirrors	11.161.074	2,06	0,14	0,00	0,6	0,00	0	0,0	5	0	1,09
32	The Sisterhood of the Traveling Pants 2	10.678.430	2,04	2,23	0,00	0,0	3,52	4,25	1,1	0	1	1,51
33	The Women	10.115.121	1,08	0,14	2,46	0,0	0,00	3,5	0,0	7	5	2,38
34	X-Files: I Want To Believe	10.021.753	3,57	0,45	3,16	1,2	0,00	0	1,5	7	7	3,04
35	Traitor	10.006.327	2,98	1,83	0,00	0,0	5,12	0	2,5	5	0	2,08
36	My Best Friend's Girl	8.265.357	1,51	0,62	0,00	0,0	0,00	1	1,9	7	1	1,68
37	Igor	7.803.347	3,24	3,06	0,00	0,0	0,00	5,4	2,7	4	0	2,17

Position	Film	Release Weekend's Box Office	Official Website	Social Network Websites	Syndicated Content	Mobile Mktg	Advergaming	Cross Brand Mktg	Viral Mktg	SEM	Widget Mktg	TOTAL SCORE
38	Bangkok Dangerous	7.783.266	1,99	0,14	0,00	0,0	4,88	0	0,0	4	0	1,34
39	Space Chimps	7.181.374	2,52	0,14	0,00	0,0	4,88	4,15	1,7	7	0	2,37
40	Disaster Movie	6.945.535	1,52	0,43	0,00	0,0	2,16	0	1,3	7	0	1,59
41	Fireproof	6.804.764	3,45	0,15	4,78	0,0	4,40	5,05	0,0	7	4	3,45
42	Swing Vote	6.230.669	1,01	0,14	0,00	0,0	4,88	0	2,5	0	0	0,84
43	Ghost Town	5.012.315	1,54	0,14	0,00	0,0	0,00	0	0,0	5	0	0,96
44	The Express	4.562.675	1,99	0,14	0,00	0,0	0,00	0	0,0	5	5,5	1,70
45	The Longshots	4.080.687	0,50	0,00	0,00	0,0	0,00	0	0,0	5	0	0,78
46	Vicky Cristina Barcelona	3.755.575	0,60	0,16	0,00	0,0	0,00	3,35	1,5	7	0	1,53
47	An American Carol	3.656.000	1,57	0,87	0,00	2,1	0,00	2,35	4,0	3	0	1,49
48	Miracle at St. Anna	3.477.996	1,03	0,14	0,00	0,0	0,00	0	0,0	7	0	1,16
49	Religulous	3.409.643	1,11	0,14	0,00	0,0	0,00	0	0,0	7	0	1,17
50	City of Ember	3.129.473	1,55	0,42	2,79	0,0	4,64	0	3,5	7	5,5	3,01
51	The Rocker	2.636.048	2,00	3,15	0,00	1,2	4,64	3,85	2,5	7	0	2,75
52	College	2.619.730	3,20	3,40	0,00	0,0	4,64	4,35	0,0	4	6	3,01
53	Flash of Genius	2.251.075	2,00	0,14	0,00	0,0	0,00	0	0,0	5	5,5	1,70
54	Blindness	1.950.260	2,60	0,14	4,12	0,0	0,00	0	2,3	5	0	1,83
55	How to Lose Friends & Alienate People	1.430.294	2,47	2,72	3,11	0,0	3,28	0	2,5	5	6	3,04
56	Choke	1.319.286	3,03	0,14	1,97	0,0	0,00	3	2,5	5	2,5	2,23

Position	Film	Release Weekend's Box Office	Official Website	Social Network Websites	Syndicated Content	Mobile Mktg	Adverga ming	Cross Brand Mktg	Viral Mktg	SEM	Widget Mktg	TOTAL SCORE
57	Henry Poole Is Here	805.219	1,04	0,56	0,00	0,0	0,00	0	0,0	5	0	0,93
58	Hamlet 2	439.925	3,02	0,14	0,54	0,0	0,00	2,5	0,0	5	0	1,49
59	Brideshead revisited	339.616	1,51	0,14	0,00	0,0	0,00	0	0,0	0	0	0,26
60	Bottle Shock	277.839	2,54	0,42	0,00	0,0	0,00	0	0,0	7	0	1,44
61	Appaloosa	248.847	1,48	0,00	0,00	0,0	0,00	2,4	0,0	4	0	1,01
62	Kit Kittredge: An American Girl	220.297	2,52	0,14	1,11	0,0	2,40	4	0,0	5	0	1,83
63	Beer for My Horses	209.253	0,50	0,00	0,00	0,0	0,00	0	0,0	7	0	1,06
64	The Duchess	190.426	1,54	0,42	0,00	0,0	0,00	2,5	0,0	7	0	1,50
65	Tell No One	169.707	0,99	0,00	0,00	0,0	0,00	0	0,0	5	0	0,86
66	Man On Wire	51.392	0,61	0,14	0,00	0,0	0,00	0	0,0	7	0	1,09

Release Weekend's Box Office Ranking

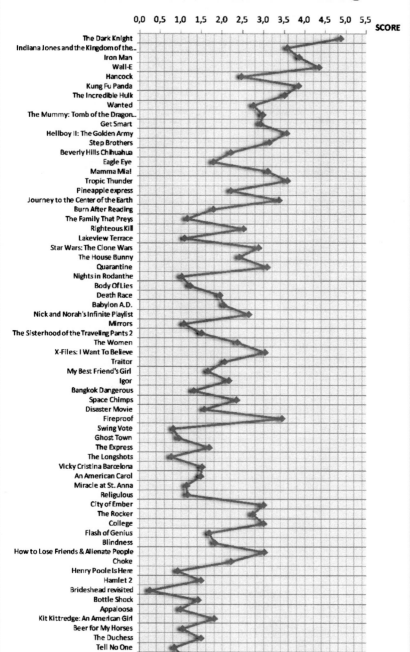

Exhibit 4 – Production Budget Ranking

Position	Film	Production Budget	Online Marketing Score
1	The Dark Knight	185.000.000	4,89
2	Indiana Jones and the Kingdom of the Crystal Skull	185.000.000	3,59
3	Wall-E	180.000.000	4,35
4	Hancock	150.000.000	2,49
5	The Incredible Hulk	150.000.000	3,53
6	The Mummy: Tomb of the Dragon Emperor	145.000.000	2,99
7	Iron Man	140.000.000	3,89
8	Kung Fu Panda	130.000.000	3,87
9	Eagle Eye	105.000.000	1,81
10	Tropic Thunder	92.000.000	3,59
11	Get Smart	80.000.000	2,94
12	Wanted	75.000.000	2,78
13	Hellboy II: The Golden Army	72.000.000	3,58
14	Body Of Lies	70.000.000	1,24
15	Step Brothers	65.000.000	3,16
16	Righteous Kill	60.000.000	2,54
17	Babylon A.D.	60.000.000	2,06
18	Mamma Mia!	52.000.000	3,12
19	Journey to the Center of the Earth	45.000.000	3,38
20	Death Race	45.000.000	1,96
21	My Best Friend's Girl	45.000.000	1,68
22	Miracle at St. Anna	45.000.000	1,16
23	Bangkok Dangerous	40.000.000	1,34
24	The Express	40.000.000	1,70
25	City of Ember	38.000.000	3,01
26	Burn After Reading	37.000.000	1,81
27	Space Chimps	37.000.000	2,37
28	Mirrors	35.000.000	1,09
29	X-Files: I Want To Believe	30.000.000	3,04
30	Igor	30.000.000	2,17
31	How to Lose Friends & Alienate People	28.000.000	3,04
32	The Sisterhood of the Traveling Pants 2	27.000.000	1,51

33	Pineapple express	25.000.000	**2,23**
34	The House Bunny	25.000.000	**2,44**
35	Disaster Movie	25.000.000	**1,59**
36	Blindness	25.000.000	**1,83**
37	Lakeview Terrace	22.000.000	**1,11**
38	Traitor	22.000.000	**2,08**
39	Swing Vote	21.000.000	**0,84**
40	Ghost Town	20.000.000	**0,96**
41	An American Carol	20.000.000	**1,49**
42	Flash of Genius	20.000.000	**1,70**
43	Brideshead revisited	20.000.000	**0,26**
44	Appaloosa	20.000.000	**1,01**
45	The Women	16.500.000	**2,38**
46	Vicky Cristina Barcelona	15.500.000	**1,53**
47	The Rocker	15.000.000	**2,75**
48	Quarantine	12.000.000	**3,11**
49	Tell No One	11.700.000	**0,86**
50	Kit Kittredge: An American Girl	10.000.000	**1,83**
51	Nick and Norah's Infinite Playlist	9.000.000	**2,66**
52	Hamlet 2	9.000.000	**1,49**
53	Choke	8.500.000	**2,23**
54	College	6.500.000	**3,01**
55	Religulous	2.500.000	**1,17**
56	Fireproof	500.000	**3,45**

Exhibit 5 – Cumulative Box Office after 3 Weeks Ranking

Position	Film	Cumulative Box Office after 3weeks	Final Score
1	The Dark Knight	393.751.065	4,89
2	Indiana Jones and the Kingdom of the Crystal Skull	253.014.750	3,59
3	Iron Man	223.124.385	3,89
4	Hancock	191.543.979	2,49
5	Wall-E	163.055.900	4,35
6	Kung Fu Panda	155.830.875	3,87
7	The Incredible Hulk	115.859.210	3,53
8	Wanted	112.455.060	2,78
9	Get Smart	98.100.652	2,94
10	Mamma Mia!	87.470.125	3,12
11	Tropic Thunder	86.935.945	3,59
12	The Mummy: Tomb of the Dragon Emperor	86.245.775	2,99
13	Step Brothers	81.132.136	3,16
14	Pineapple express	73.780.191	2,23
15	Eagle Eye	70.409.979	1,81
16	Beverly Hills Chihuahua	69.282.560	2,23
17	Hellboy II: The Golden Army	66.059.925	3,58
18	Journey to the Center of the Earth	60.487.455	3,38
19	Burn After Reading	45.567.391	1,81
20	The Sisterhood of the Traveling Pants 2	38.319.055	1,51
21	The House Bunny	36.611.667	2,44
22	Righteous Kill	34.711.327	2,54
23	The Family That Preys	32.761.276	1,17
24	Nights in Rodanthe	32.297.101	1,03
25	Lakeview Terrace	32.201.255	1,11
26	Body Of Lies	30.890.000	1,24
27	Star Wars: The Clone Wars	30.672.432	2,90
28	Death Race	29.909.125	1,96
29	Quarantine	28.770.000	3,11
30	Nick and Norah's Infinite Playlist	26.500.875	2,66
31	Mirrors	25.395.133	1,09
32	The Women	24.072.805	2,38
33	Space Chimps	21.971.016	2,37

34	Traitor	20.734.170	2,08
35	Babylon A.D.	20.415.057	2,06
36	X-Files: I Want To Believe	19.750.553	3,04
37	My Best Friend's Girl	17.610.847	1,68
38	Igor	17.073.170	2,17
39	Fireproof	16.875.765	3,45
40	Swing Vote	14.687.549	0,84
41	Bangkok Dangerous	14.535.371	1,34
42	Vicky Cristina Barcelona	13.309.881	1,53
43	Disaster Movie	12.655.988	1,59
44	Ghost Town	11.526.769	0,96
45	The Longshots	9.893.428	0,78
46	The Express	9.330.000	1,70
47	Religulous	9.068.325	1,17
48	Miracle at St. Anna	7.441.895	1,16
49	City of Ember	6.876.000	3,01
50	An American Carol	6.776.000	1,49
51	The Rocker	6.156.842	2,75
52	Kit Kittredge: An American Girl	5.822.544	1,83
53	Appaloosa	5.605.167	1,01
54	College	4.600.628	3,01
55	Hamlet 2	4.359.680	1,49
56	Flash of Genius	4.234.040	1,70
57	Brideshead revisited	3.346.544	0,26
58	Blindness	3.073.393	1,83
59	How to Lose Friends & Alienate People	2.725.950	3,04
60	Choke	2.703.319	2,23
61	The Duchess	1.950.786	1,50
62	Bottle Shock	1.671.490	1,44
63	Henry Poole Is Here	1.646.452	0,93
64	Tell No One	1.057.050	0,86
65	Man On Wire	435.943	1,09
66	Beer for My Horses	411.212	1,06

Exhibit 6 – Genre Analysis

FILM	GENRE	Official Website	Social Network	Syndicated Content	Mobile Mktg	Advergaming	Cross Brand Mktg	Viral Mktg	SEM	Widget Mktg	Final Score
Babylon A.D.	action	1,06	1,64	1,44	-	3,28	-	-	7,00	2,00	2,06
Bangkok Dangerous	action	1,99	0,14	-	-	4,88	-	-	4,00	-	1,34
Death Race	action	2,57	0,18	-	1,60	4,40	-	3,50	5,00	-	1,96
Get Smart	action	3,98	3,98	1,80	2,10	2,16	5,20	1,10	5,00	-	2,94
Hancock	action	2,34	2,32	-	0,70	5,12	-	2,50	4,00	4,50	2,49
Hellboy II: The Golden Army	action	5,32	1,63	-	4,20	2,76	1,70	3,50	7,00	4,50	3,58
Indiana Jones and the Kingdom of the Crystal Skull	action	5,04	4,77	-	2,20	-	3,35	-	7,00	6,50	3,59
Iron Man	action	4,20	3,62	-	2,60	-	5,80	3,50	7,00	6,50	3,89
Journey to the Center of the Earth	action	2,60	-	2,17	-	5,12	4,20	2,50	7,00	5,50	3,38
Pineapple express	action	2,09	3,15	-	1,20	2,16	-	-	5,00	4,50	2,23
Star Wars: The Clone Wars	action	3,12	-	-	-	4,88	1,55	-	7,00	7,00	2,90
The Dark Knight	action	5,52	4,70	-	7,00	5,80	5,30	6,20	7,00	3,50	4,89
The Incredible Hulk	action	4,65	2,38	-	0,60	4,40	4,70	-	7,00	5,50	3,53
The Mummy: Tomb of the Dragon Emperor	action	3,51	0,15	3,21	3,10	4,40	3,50	-	7,00	1,00	2,99
Tropic Thunder	action	2,86	3,85	-	2,40	3,52	-	5,40	7,00	6,00	3,59
Wanted	action	4,00	3,66	-	1,00	4,88	3,50	3,50	4,00	-	2,78
Beverly Hills Chihuahua	adventure	2,54	-	-	1,80	2,16	-	5,80	7,00	-	2,23
City of Ember	adventure	1,55	0,42	2,79	-	4,64	-	3,50	7,00	5,50	3,01

Igor	animation	3,24	3,06	-	-	-	5,40	2,70	4,00	-	**2,17**
Kung Fu Panda	animation	4,12	2,56	0,30	3,10	5,36	5,85	-	7,00	5,50	**3,87**
Space Chimps	animation	2,52	0,14	-	-	4,88	4,15	1,70	7,00	-	**2,37**
Wall-E	animation	4,44	2,57	0,60	6,30	5,60	5,00	2,50	7,00	5,50	**4,35**
An American Carol	comedy	1,57	0,87	-	2,10	-	2,35	4,00	3,00	-	**1,49**
...er for My Horses	comedy	0,50	-	-	-	-	-	-	7,00	-	**1,06**
...urn After Reading	comedy	1,50	2,31	-	0,60	1,04	-	-	4,00	5,00	**1,81**
Choke	comedy	3,03	0,14	1,97	-	-	3,00	2,50	5,00	2,50	**2,23**
College	comedy	3,20	3,40	-	-	4,64	4,35	-	4,00	6,00	**3,01**
Disaster Movie	comedy	1,52	0,43	-	-	2,16	-	1,30	7,00	-	**1,59**
Ghost Town	comedy	1,54	0,14	-	-	-	-	-	5,00	-	**0,96**
Hamlet 2	comedy	3,02	0,14	0,54	-	-	2,50	-	5,00	-	**1,49**
Henry Poole Is Here	comedy	1,04	0,56	-	-	-	-	-	5,00	-	**0,93**
How to Lose Friends & Alienate People	comedy	2,47	2,72	3,11	-	3,28	-	2,50	5,00	6,00	**3,04**
Mamma Mia!	comedy	3,91	0,81	-	-	3,76	4,20	0,50	7,00	5,50	**3,12**
My Best Friend's Girl	comedy	1,51	0,62	-	-	-	1,00	1,90	7,00	1,00	**1,68**
Step Brothers	comedy	2,54	3,46	-	2,30	2,40	-	4,20	7,00	5,00	**3,16**
...ving Vote	comedy	1,01	0,14	-	-	4,88	-	2,50	-	-	**0,84**
...he House Bunny	comedy	1,53	2,91	-	2,40	3,76	3,50	0,50	7,00	-	**2,44**

The Rocker	comedy	2,00	3,15	-	1,20	4,64	3,85	2,50	7,00	-	**2,75**
The Women	comedy	1,08	0,14	2,46	-	-	3,50	-	7,00	5,00	**2,38**
Vicky Cristina Barcelona	comedy	0,60	0,16	-	-	-	3,35	1,50	7,00	-	**1,53**
Righteous Kill	crime	2,08	0,14	-	2,10	3,52	1,00	-	7,00	5,50	**2,54**
Man On Wire	documentary	0,61	0,14	-	-	-	-	-	7,00	-	**1,09**
Religulous	documentary	1,11	0,14	-	-	-	-	-	7,00	-	**1,17**
Blindness	drama	2,60	0,14	4,12	-	-	-	2,30	5,00	-	**1,83**
Body Of Lies	drama	1,51	0,14	-	-	-	-	-	7,00	-	**1,24**
Bottle Shock	drama	2,54	0,42	-	-	-	-	-	7,00	-	**1,44**
Brideshead revisited	drama	1,51	0,14	-	-	-	-	-	-	-	**0,26**
Eagle Eye	drama	1,69	1,85	-	2,80	4,64	-	-	5,00	-	**1,81**
Fireproof	drama	3,45	0,15	4,78	-	4,40	5,05	-	7,00	4,00	**3,45**
Flash of Genius	drama	2,00	0,14	-	-	-	-	-	5,00	5,50	**1,70**
Kit Kittredge: An American Girl	drama	2,52	0,14	1,11	-	2,40	4,00	-	5,00	-	**1,83**
Lakeview Terrace	drama	1,01	0,42	-	-	2,16	-	-	5,00	-	**1,11**
Miracle at St. Anna	drama	1,03	0,14	-	-	-	-	-	7,00	-	**1,16**
Nick and Norah's Infinite Playlist	drama	2,52	3,23	-	1,50	-	3,85	-	5,00	6,00	**2,66**
Nights in Rodanthe	drama	0,55	-	-	-	-	2,70	-	5,00	-	**1,03**
Tell No One	drama	0,99	-	-	-	-	-	-	5,00	-	**0,86**
The Duchess	drama	1,54	0,42	-	-	-	2,50	-	7,00	-	**1,50**

The Express	drama	1,99	0,14	-	-	-	-	-	5,00	5,50	**1,70**
The Family That Preys	drama	1,47	-	-	-	2,16	-	0,50	5,00	-	**1,17**
The Longshots	drama	0,50	-	-	-	-	-	-	5,00	-	**0,78**
The Sisterhood of the Traveling Pants 2	drama	2,04	2,23	-	-	3,52	4,25	1,10	-	1,00	**1,51**
Traitor	drama	2,98	1,83	-	-	5,12	-	2,50	5,00	-	**2,08**
Mirrors	horror	2,06	0,14	-	0,60	-	-	-	5,00	-	**1,09**
Quarantine	horror	2,50	3,33	-	-	4,40	1,85	2,50	7,00	4,50	**3,11**
X-Files: I Want To Believe	mystery	3,57	0,45	3,16	1,20	-	-	1,50	7,00	7,00	**3,04**
Appaloosa	western	1,48	-	-	-	-	2,40	-	4,00	-	**1,01**

Table of Figures

Bibliography

Ahern, M. (2008, June 19). *4 winning widget strategies.* Retrieved from iMedia Connection: http://www.imediaconnection.com/content/marketing-channels-desktop-apps-4-winning-widget-strategies_19692.html

Alexa. (n.d.). *About the Alexa Traffic Rankings.* Retrieved from Alexa: http://www.alexa.com/site/help/traffic_learn_more

Bader, J. (n.d.). *How to Create Profits Using Viral Marketing Techniques.* Retrieved from MRP Web Media: http://www.mrpwebmedia.com/articles/viralmarketing.html

Balter, D. (2008). *The Word of Mouth Manuale, Volume II.* Boston: BzzAgent.

BBC. (2005, July 19). *News Corp in $580m internet buy.* Retrieved from BBC: http://news.bbc.co.uk/1/hi/business/4695495.stm

Bedell, D. (1998, October 27). *Meeting your new best friends Six Degrees widens your contacts in exchange for sampling Web sites.* Retrieved from The Dallas Morning News: http://www.dougbedell.com/sixdegrees1.html

Beirne, M. (2008, September 15). *Nielsen: Gamers Responding Favorably to In-Game Ads.* Retrieved from MediaWeek: http://www.mediaweek.com/mw/content_display/news/digital-downloads/gaming/e3ibd93dba87a9330a3522234ad93cb35e4

Bhopu. (2007, November 13). *Emergence of Social Networks and its impact on New Media.* Retrieved from Bhopu: http://bhopu.com/2007/11/13/Emergence-of-Social-Networks-and-its-impact-on-New-Media

Borland, J. (2005, February 28). *Blurring the line between games and life.* Retrieved from CNET: http://news.cnet.com/Blurring-the-line-between-games-and-life/2100-1024_3-5590956.html

Bourke, C. (2006). *How to Develop a Mobile Marketing Strategy.* London: Aerodeon.

Boyd, D. (2004). Friendster and Publicly Articulated Social Networking. *Conference on Human Factors and Computing Systems.* Wien.

Boyd, d., & Ellison, N. (2007). Social network sites: Definition, history, and scholarship. *13(1)* . Journal of Computer-Mediated Communication. Retrieved from Journal of Computer-Mediated Communication: http://jcmc.indiana.edu/vol13/issue1/boyd.ellison.html

Brodesser-Akner, C. (2008, April 17). *Movie Tie-Ins Coming Soon to Everywhere Near You.* Retrieved from Advertising Age: http://www.commercialexploitation.org/news/movietieins.htm

Buckner, K., Fang, H., & Quiao, S. (2002, February). *Advergaming: A New Genre in Internet Advertising.* Retrieved from http://www.dcs.napier.ac.uk/~mm/socbytes/feb2002_i/9.html

BusinessWeek. (2007, November 12). *So Many Ads, So Few Clicks.* Retrieved from BusinessWeek: http://www.businessweek.com/magazine/content/07_46/b4058053.htm?campaign_id=rss_dai ly

Carton, S. (2005, March 21). *Alternate Reality Gaming and You.* Retrieved from ClickZ: http://www.clickz.com/showPage.html?page=3491191

Cavalli, E. (2008, June 17). *Study: 82 Percent of Consumers Accept In-Game Ads.* Retrieved from Wired: http://blog.wired.com/games/2008/06/study-82-percen.html

Celata, G., & Caruso, S. (2003). *Cinema industria e marketing.* Milano: Edizioni Angelo Guerini e Associati.

Chen, J., & Ringel, M. (2001). *Can Advergaming be the Future of Interactive Advertising?* New York: KPE.

Colantonio, F. (n.d.). *Nuove tendenze nel fashion marketing: gli Alternate-Reality Games (ARGs) e il caso EDOC Laundry.* Retrieved from NoBrandAgency: http://www.nobrandagency.com/articoli-marketing-alternativo.html

comScore. (2008, February 19). *M:METRICS REPORTS MIXED FORTUNES FOR MOBILE GAMES INDUSTRY.* Retrieved from comScore: http://www.comscore.com/press/release.asp?press=2458

comScore. (2008, August 12). *Social Networking Explodes Worldwide as Sites Increase their Focus on Cultural Relevance.* Retrieved from comScore: http://www.comscore.com/press/release.asp?press=2396

Dalli, D. (2003). Il product placement cinematografico: oltre la pubblicità? *Le tendenze del marketing* (p. 16). Venezia: Università Ca' Foscari Venezia.

Dena, C. (2008, November). *ARG Stats.* Retrieved from Christy Dena: http://www.christydena.com/online-essays/arg-stats/

Dennis, J. (2008, June 6). *Multiplex Marketing.* Retrieved from Conde Nast Portfolio: http://www.commercialexploitation.org/news/2008/06/multiplex.htm

eMarketer. (2008, May 13). *eMarketer Lowers Social Networking Ad Spend Estimate.* Retrieved from eMarketer: http://www.emarketer.com/Article.aspx?id=1006295

eMarketer. (2008, August 26). *Mobile Games Make the Next Move.* Retrieved from eMarketer: http://www.emarketer.com/Article.aspx?id=1006500

eMarketer. (2008, February 20). *Widget Wins Hinge on Social Networks.* Retrieved from eMarketer: http://www.emarketer.com/Article.aspx?id=1005962

ESA. (2008). *2008 Essential Facts About the Computer and Video Game Industry.* Entertainment Software Association.

Frank, A. (2008, August 29). *Some Perspective on Social Networks.* Retrieved from eMarketer: http://www.emarketer.com/Article.aspx?id=1006464

Gabe, G. (2006, August 10). *So Now It's Called WOM!* Retrieved from The Internet Marketing Driver: http://www.hmtweb.com/blog/2006/08/so-now-its-called-wom.html

Gabe, G. (2006, October 9). *The Difference Between Bzz Marketing, Viral Marketing, and Word of Mouth Marketing.* Retrieved from The Internet Marketing Driver: http://www.hmtweb.com/blog/2006/10/difference-between-bzz-marketing-viral.html

Godin, S. (2007, October 17). *Is viral marketing the same as word of mouth?* Retrieved from Seth Godin's Blog: http://sethgodin.typepad.com/seths_blog/2007/10/is-viral-market.html

Godin, S. (2000). *Unleashing the Ideavirus.* Do You Zoom.

Gottschalk, M. (1995, August 22). *Film's Influence On Fashion Traced In TV Documentary.* Retrieved from The Seattle Times: http://community.seattletimes.nwsource.com/archive/?date=19950822&slug=2137555

Gutnik, L., Huang, Y., Blue Lin, J., & Schmidt, T. (2007). *New Trends in Product Placement.* Berkeley: University of Berkeley.

Hallerman, D. (2008, January). *Search Engine Marketing:.* Retrieved from eMarketer: http://www.emarketer.com/Report.aspx?code=emarketer_2000473

Hallerman, D. (2008, March). *US Online Advertising: Resilient in a Rough Economy.* Retrieved from eMarketer: http://www.emarketer.com/Report.aspx?code=2000488

Hamburg, M. (2008, May 27). *Alternate Reality Games – Playing with Marketing.* Retrieved from One Degree: http://www.onedegree.ca/2008/05/alternate-reali.html

Handy, A. (2005, May 18). *The Buzzmakers.* Retrieved from East Bay Express: http://www.eastbayexpress.com/gyrobase/the_buzzmakers/Content?oid=289223&page=1

HitWise. (2008, July 23). *Facebook sees 40 Percent Growth Year over Year.* Retrieved from HitWise: http://www.hitwise.com/press-center/hitwiseHS2004/us-facebook-grows-40-percent-23072008.php

HitWise. (2008, August 15). *Top US domains by traffic in June 2008.* Retrieved from ITfacts: http://www.itfacts.biz/top-us-domains-by-traffic-in-june-2008/11192

Holahan, C. (2008, August 13). *Facebook: No. 1 Globally.* Retrieved from Business Week: http://www.businessweek.com/technology/content/aug2008/tc20080812_853725.htm

Hon, A. (2005, May 9). *The Rise of ARGs.* Retrieved from Gamasutra: http://www.gamasutra.com/features/20050509/hon_01.shtml

IAB & Microsoft. (2008). *Movie Marketing Online.* Internet Advertising Bureau.

IGDA. (2006). *2006 Alternate Reality Games White Paper.* IGDA.org.

Interactive Advertising Bureau. (2008). *User Generated Content, Social Media,and Advertising - An Overview.* Interactive Advertising Bureau.

Jurvetson, S., & Draper, T. (2001, May 1). *Viral Marketing phenomenon explained.* Retrieved from Draper Fisher Jurvetson: http://www.dfj.com/news/article_26.shtml

Kafka, P. (2008, September 18). *comScore August Report Card: Google Gaining, Of Course (GOOG).* Retrieved from Silicon Alley Insider: http://www.alleyinsider.com/2008/9/comscore-august-report-card-google-gaining-of-course-goog-

Kunz, B. (2008, March 3). *Why Widgets Don't Work.* Retrieved from Business Week: http://www.businessweek.com/technology/content/feb2008/tc20080229_131531.htm

Lal, R. (2007, August 11). *What is a Web Widget ?* Retrieved from Widgets for Web 2.0: http://widgets-gadgets.com/2007/08/what-is-web-widget.html

Lee, C. (2005, June 16). Blogs the latest twist in the film marketing game. *Los Angeles Times* .

Lenssen, P. (2006, April 12). *Google's Da Vinci Code Quest.* Retrieved from Google Blogoscoped: http://blogoscoped.com/archive/2006-04-12-n31.html

Leo, A. (2006, August 15). *If Samuel L. Jackson Called, Would You See His Movie?* Retrieved from ABC News: http://abcnews.go.com/Business/story?id=2313405&page=1

Loewenhagen, R. (n.d.). *Advergaming: Advertising through Video Games.* Retrieved from www.LivingMyLifestyle.net: http://www.livingmylifestyle.net/articles/rloewenhagen/Advergaming_or_Advertising_through _Video_Games/

Magzan, L. (2002, November 25). *The business of Bond...James Bond.* Retrieved from CNN Money: http://money.cnn.com/2002/11/21/news/james_bond/index.htm

Manjoo, M. (2002, May 9). *Flash: Blogging Goes Corporate.* Retrieved from WIRED: http://www.wired.com/culture/lifestyle/news/2002/05/52380

MarketingTerms.com. (n.d.). *Search Engine Optimization.* Retrieved from Marketing Terms: http://www.marketingterms.com/dictionary/search_engine_optimization/

McGonigal, J. (2003). *'This Is Not a Game': Immersive Aesthetics and Collective Play.* Department of Theater, Dance & Performance Studies. Berkeley: University of California at Berkeley.

Meattle, J. (2007, February 26). *Top-20 Domains ranked by Attention Share: Yahoo gained, Most e-commerce sites lost.* Retrieved from Compete: http://blog.compete.com/2007/02/26/top-20-domains-attention-share-time-spent-yahoo-gain/

Microsoft RSS Blog. (2005, December 14). *Icons: It's still orange.* Retrieved from Microsoft RSS Blog: http://blogs.msdn.com/rssteam/archive/2005/12/14/503778.aspx

Microsoft. (n.d.). *Stay up to date with Microsoft RSS Feeds.* Retrieved from Microsoft: http://www.microsoft.com/windows/rss/default.mspx

Mobile Marketing Association. (2008, July 30). *Universal Pictures Launches "Forgetting Sarah Marshall" SMS Ad Campaign.* Retrieved from Mobile Marketing Association: http://mmaglobal.com/modules/article/view.article.php/2042

Montgomery, A. (2001). Applying Quantitative Marketing Techniques. *Interfaces*, *31* (2), pp. 93-108.

MPAA. (2008). *Entertainment Industry Market Statistics, 2007.* http://www.mpaa.org.

MPAA. (2008). *Movie Attendance Study, 2007.* http://www.mpaa.org.

Nelson, P. (1970). Information and consumer behavior. *Journal of Political Economy*, *78* (2), pp. 311-329.

Nichols, J. (2008). *Fundamentals of Mobile Marketing.* Catalyst SF.

Nielsen. (2008, July). *Critical Mass - The Worldwide State of the Mobile Web.* Retrieved from Nielsen Mobile: www.nielsenmobile.com/documents/CriticalMass.pdf

Nielsen Entertainment. (2007, August 8). *In-Game Ads Can Increase Brand Familiarity 64%, Purchase Consideration 41%.* Retrieved from Marketing Charts: http://www.marketingcharts.com/interactive/in-game-ads-can-increase-brand-familiarity-64-purchase-consideration-41-1229/

Nielsen Games. (2008, June 18). *82% of Gamers React Positively to Contextual In-Game Ads.* Retrieved from Marketing Charts.

Nielsen, J. (2007, August 20). *Banner Blindness: Old and New Findings.* Retrieved from Alertbox: http://www.useit.com/alertbox/banner-blindness.html

Nudd, T. (2005, August 26). *'Ring Two' viral so good it's scary.* Retrieved from AdFreak: http://adweek.blogs.com/adfreak/2005/08/ring_two_viral_.html

Obringer, L. (n.d.). *How Advergaming Works.* Retrieved from howstuffworks: http://money.howstuffworks.com/advergaming.htm

OECD. (2007). *PARTICIPATIVE WEB: USER-CREATED CONTENT.* Directorate for science, technology and industry, Committee for information, computer and communications policy. Organisation for Economic Co-operation and Development.

O'Reilly, T. (2005, September 30). *What Is Web 2.0.* Retrieved from O'Reilly: http://www.oreillynet.com/pub/a/oreilly/tim/news/2005/09/30/what-is-web-20.html

OTX. (2007, September 17). *Buzz a Major Influencer of Teens' Movie-Going Decisions.* Retrieved from MarketingCharts: http://www.marketingcharts.com/outdoor/buzz-a-major-influencer-of-teens-movie-going-decisions-1666/

Owyang, J. (2008, January 29). *Case Study: How Sony Leveraged A Popular "Vampire" Facebook Widget To Reach It's Community.* Retrieved from Web Strategy by Jeremiah: http://www.web-strategist.com/blog/2008/01/29/case-study-how-sony-leveraged-a-popular-vampire-facebook-widget-to-reach-its-community/

Owyang, J. (n.d.). *Social Networking.* Retrieved from Web Strategy by Jeremiah: http://www.web-strategist.com/blog/category/social-networking/

Oxford University Press. (n.d.). *Podcast.* Retrieved from Oxford University Press: http://www.oup.com/elt/catalogue/teachersites/oald7/wotm/wotm_archive/podcast?cc=glob al

PC Magazine. (n.d.). *Definition of: social networking site.* Retrieved from PC Magazine: http://www.pcmag.com/encyclopedia_term/0,2542,t=social+networking+site&i=55316,00.asp

PC Magazine. (n.d.). *Podcast.* Retrieved from PC Magazine: http://www.pcmag.com/encyclopedia_term/0,2542,t=podcast&i=49433,00.asp

PCMagazine. (n.d.). *Definition of RSS.* Retrieved from PCMagazine: http://www.pcmag.com/encyclopedia_term/0,2542,t=RSS&i=50680,00.asp

PEW/INTERNET. (2008, July 22). *Demographics of Internet Users.* Retrieved from Pew/Internet: http://www.pewinternet.org/trends/User_Demo_7.22.08.htm

PEW/INTERNET. (2008). *Writing, Technology and Teens.* http://www.pewinternet.org.

Pham, A., & Watson, N. (1993). *The Film Marketing Handbook.* Hampshire: Media Business School.

Phillips, L. (2008, October 23). *US Internet User Update.* Retrieved from eMarketer: http://www.emarketer.com/Article.aspx?id=1006655

Phillips, S. (2007, July 25). *A brief history of Facebook.* Retrieved from guardian.co.uk: http://www.guardian.co.uk/technology/2007/jul/25/media.newmedia

Pine II, B., & Gilmore, J. (1999). *The Experience Economy.* Boston: Harvard Business School Press.

Pishevar, S. (2006, September 12). *Widget Marketing: Engage Audiences.* Retrieved from iMedia Connection: http://www.imediaconnection.com/printpage/printpage.aspx?id=11135

Podcast Alley. (n.d.). *What is a podcast.* Retrieved from Podcast Alley: http://www.podcastalley.com/what_is_a_podcast.php

Radd, D. (2008, August 13). *Tropic Thunder's Perfect Storm of Cross-Promotion.* Retrieved from Business Week: http://www.businessweek.com/innovate/content/aug2008/id20080813_874599.htm

Rayport, J. (1996, December). *The Virus of Marketing.* Retrieved from Fast Company: http://www.fastcompany.com/magazine/06/virus.html

Rose, F. (2007, December 20). *Secret Websites, Coded Messages: The New World of Immersive Games.* Retrieved from Wired: http://www.wired.com/entertainment/music/magazine/16-01/ff_args

RSS Specifications. (n.d.). *History of RSS.* Retrieved from RSS Specifications: http://www.rss-specifications.com/history-rss.htm

Saleem, M. (2007, December 26). *Alternate Reality Games: What Makes or Breaks Them?* Retrieved from Read Write Web: http://www.readwriteweb.com/archives/alternate_reality_games_viral_marketing.php

Salvemini, S. (2002). *Il cinema impresa possibile*. Milano: EGEA.

Salvemini, S. (1992). Tra cultura e mercati: cenni sull'industria cinematografica. *Economia della Cultura* (1), pp. 49-55.

Salvemini, S., & Soda, G. (2001). *Artwork & Network*. Milano: EGEA.

Sauer, A. (2005, September 29). *Product Placement: Making the Most of a Close-Up*. Retrieved from Business Week:
http://www.businessweek.com/innovate/content/sep2005/id20050929_293062.htm

Schiller, G. (2005, September 7). *Attention-grabbing Film Promotions Were The Exception And Not The Rule*. Retrieved from The Hollywood Reporter:
http://www.allbusiness.com/services/motion-pictures/4916784-1.html

SearchCIO-Midmarket. (n.d.). *Search Engine Optimization*. Retrieved from SearchCIO-Midmarket:
http://searchcio-midmarket.techtarget.com/sDefinition/0,,sid183_gci1003465,00.html

SEMPO. (2008). *The State of Search Engine Marketing 2007*. sempo.org.

SNLKagan. (2007, August 23). *Mobile Phone Penetration 84%, Wireless Revenue $155B by Year's End*. Retrieved from MarketingCharts: http://www.marketingcharts.com/interactive/mobile-phone-penetration-84-wireless-revenue-155b-by-years-end-1371/snl-kagan-cell-phone-penetration-usjpg/

Stanley, T. (2006, December). *EBay gets in the ring with MGM to push 'Rocky'; Partnership is part of campaign to sell movie to wide range of consumers*. Retrieved from Advertising Age:
http://findarticles.com/p/articles/mi_hb6398/is_200612/ai_n25580118

Stewart, S. (2006, June 11). *Alternate Reality Games*. Retrieved from Sean Stewart:
http://www.seanstewart.org/interactive/args/

Technorati. (2008). *State of the Blogosphere 2008*. Retrieved from Technorati:
http://www.technorati.com/blogging/state-of-the-blogosphere

Technorati. (2008). *Welcome to Technorati*. Retrieved from Technorati:
http://technoratimedia.com/about/

The Auto Channel. (2005, March 14). *Jeep and Paramount Pictures Ally to Push New Film*. Retrieved from The Auto Channel:
http://www.theautochannel.com/news/2005/03/14/010854.html

The Hollywood Reporter. (2005, April 28). *Brand Practice*. Retrieved from The Hollywood Reporter:
http://www.hollywoodreporter.com/hr/search/article_display.jsp?vnu_content_id=1000901394

Thilk, C. (2007, July 18). *Bringing widgets to your movie marketing efforts*. Retrieved from Movie Marketing Madness: http://www.moviemarketingmadness.com/blog/2007/07/18/bringing-widgets-to-your-movie-marketing-efforts/

Thilk, C. (2006, September 22). *Internet is where people go for movie information.* Retrieved from Movie Marketing Madness: http://moviemarketingmadness.blogspot.com/2006/09/internet-is-where-people-go-for-movie.html

Thilk, C. (2006, February 28). *Movie Marketing and Consumer Control: Part 2.* Retrieved from Movie Marketing Madness: http://www.moviemarketingmadness.com/blog/2006/02/28/movie-marketing-and-consumer-control-part-2/

Thilk, C. (2006, March 9). *Movie Marketing and Consumer Control: Part 3.* Retrieved from Movie Marketing Madness: http://www.moviemarketingmadness.com/blog/2006/03/09/movie-marketing-and-consumer-control-part-3/

Thilk, C. (2006, March 9). *Movie Marketing and Consumer Control: Part 3.* Retrieved from Movie Marketing Madness: http://www.moviemarketingmadness.com/blog/2006/03/09/movie-marketing-and-consumer-control-part-3/

Thilk, C. (2005, March 11). *Movie Marketing and Emerging Technology.* Retrieved from Movie Marketing Madness: http://www.moviemarketingmadness.com/blog/2005/03/11/movie-marketing-and-emerging-technology/

Thilk, C. (2007, July 25). *Movie Marketing Madness: The Simpsons Movie.* Retrieved from Movie Marketing Madness: http://www.moviemarketingmadness.com/blog/2007/07/25/movie-marketing-madness-the-simpsons-movie/

Thilk, C. (2007, August 10). *The Week in Movie Search: 8/10/07.* Retrieved from Movie Marketing Madness: http://www.moviemarketingmadness.com/blog/2007/08/10/the-week-in-movie-search-81007/

Thilk, C. (2008, February 4). *Who won the Search Bowl.* Retrieved from Movie Marketing Madness: http://www.moviemarketingmadness.com/blog/2008/02/04/who-won-the-search-bowl/

Unfiction. (n.d.). Retrieved from UnFiction: http://www.unfiction.com/glossary/

UPS. (2005, September 1). *NASCAR Fans Test Drive the UPS Truck in Videogame.* Retrieved from UPS: http://pressroom.ups.com/pressreleases/current/0,1088,4596,00.html

Van Orden, J. (n.d.). *What is a podcast.* Retrieved from How to Podcast Tutorial: http://www.how-to-podcast-tutorial.com/what-is-a-podcast.htm

Walsh, M. (2006, September 22). *Google Study: Internet Directs Moviegoers.* Retrieved from MediaPost Publications: http://www.mediapost.com/publications/index.cfm?fuseaction=Articles.showArticleHomePage&art_aid=48550

Walsh, M. (2008, March 5). *Nielsen: Improved Recall, Comfort With Mobile Ads.* Retrieved from Mobile Marketing Association: http://mmaglobal.com/modules/article/view.article.php/1908

Webopedia. (n.d.). *RSS.* Retrieved from Webopedia: http://www.webopedia.com/TERM/R/RSS.html

Webopedia. (n.d.). *Syndication.* Retrieved from Webopedia:
http://www.webopedia.com/TERM/S/syndication.html

Williamson, D. (2008, September). *College Students Online:.* Retrieved from eMarketer:
http://www.emarketer.com/Report.aspx?code=emarketer_2000524&src=report_summary_rep
ortsell

Williamson, D. (2008, February). *Web Widgets and Applications: Destination Unknown.* Retrieved
from eMarketer: http://www.emarketer.com/Reports/All/Emarketer_2000368.aspx

Word of Mouth Marketing Association. (2006). *Word of Mouth 101.* Chicago: Word of Mouth
Marketing Association.

Wortham, J. (2007, December 17). *After 10 Years of Blogs, the Future's Brighter Than Ever.*
Retrieved from Wired:
http://www.wired.com/entertainment/theweb/news/2007/12/blog_anniversary

Yared, P. (2008, February 29). *Widgets: The Future of Online Ads.* Retrieved from Business Week:
http://www.businessweek.com/technology/content/feb2008/tc20080229_871649.htm

Lightning Source UK Ltd.
Milton Keynes UK
UKOW052017310112

186425UK00001B/12/P